"This book is dedicated to all children, as they are the future of our world."

THIS BOOK BELONGS TO:

———◇————————————◇———

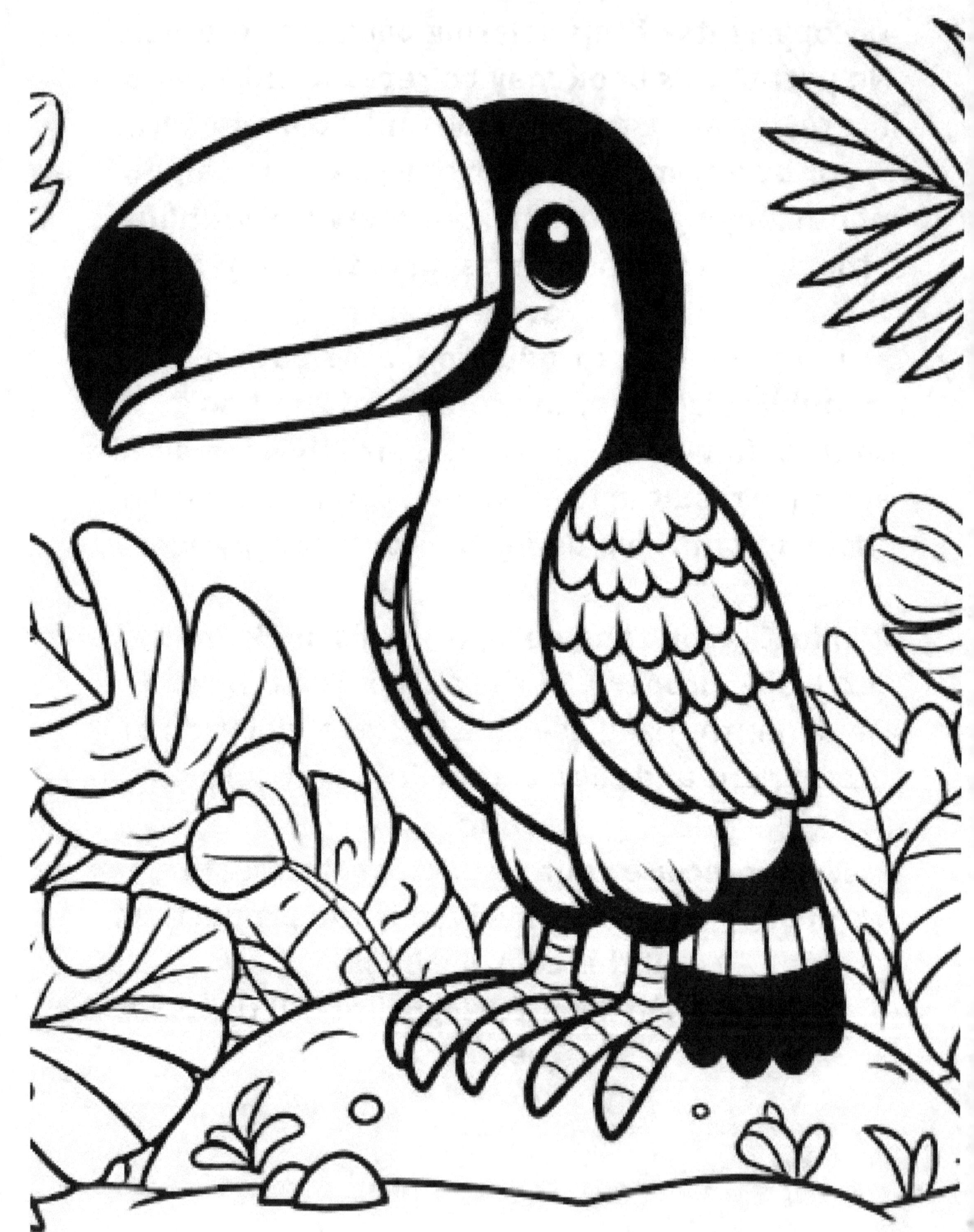

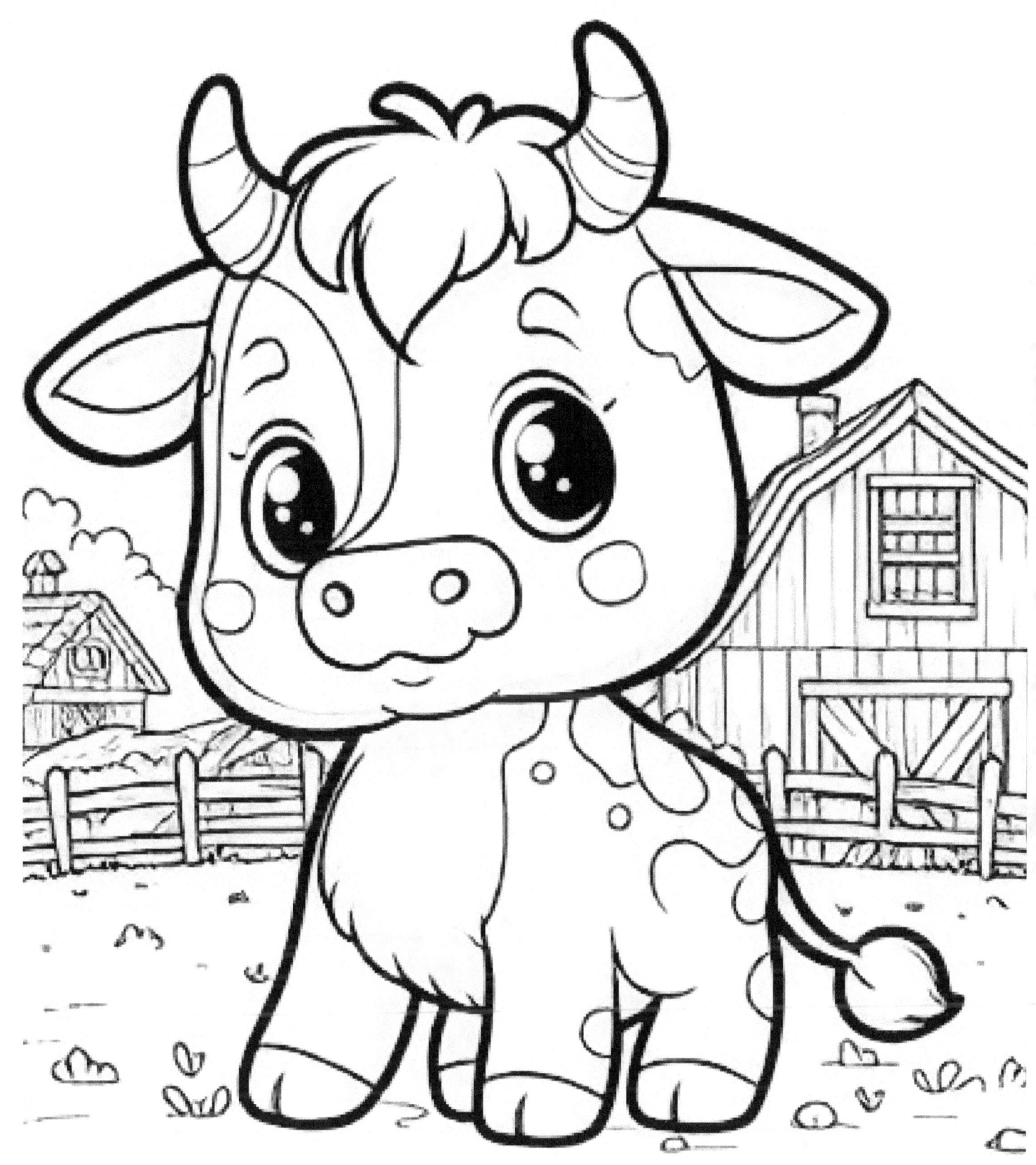

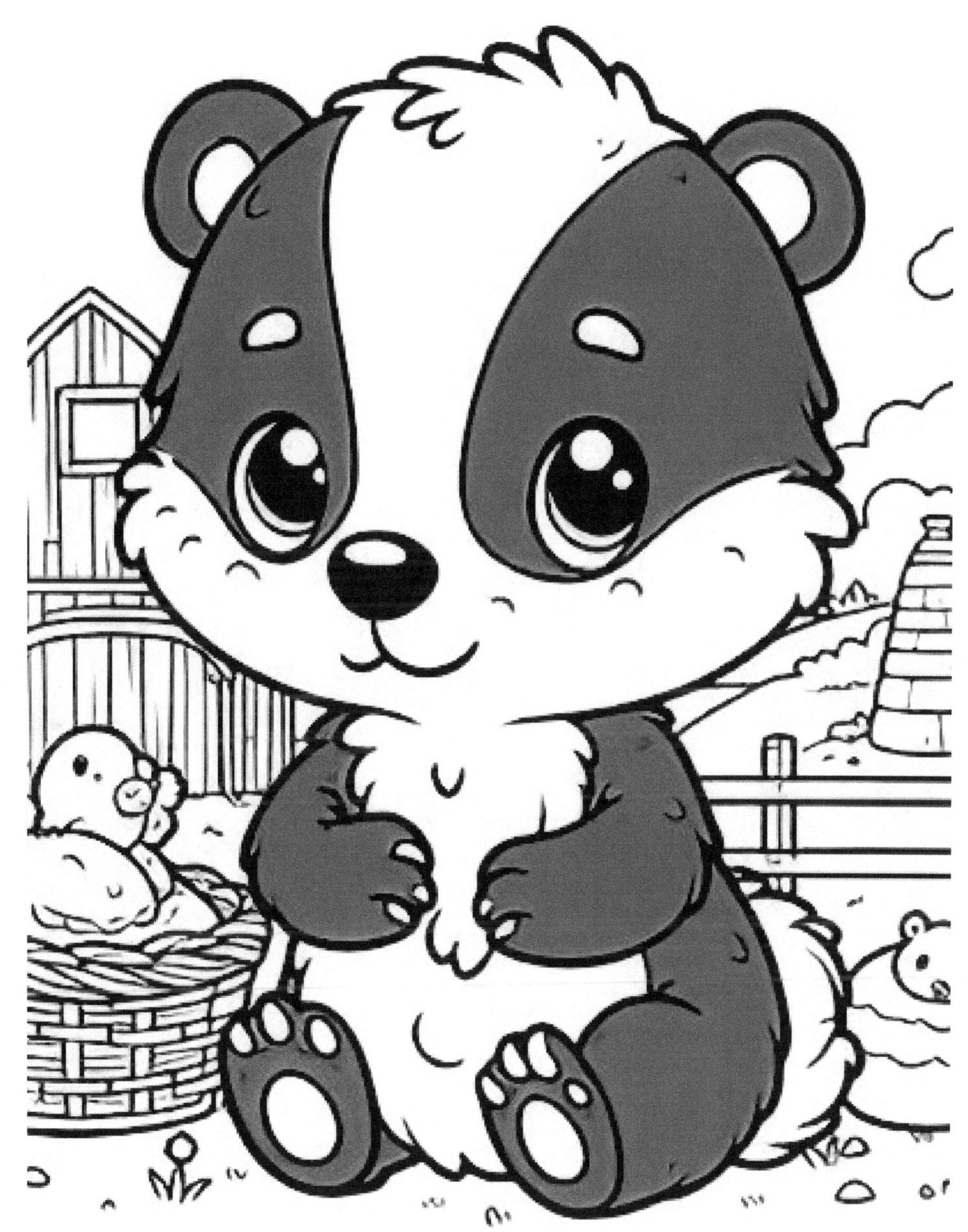

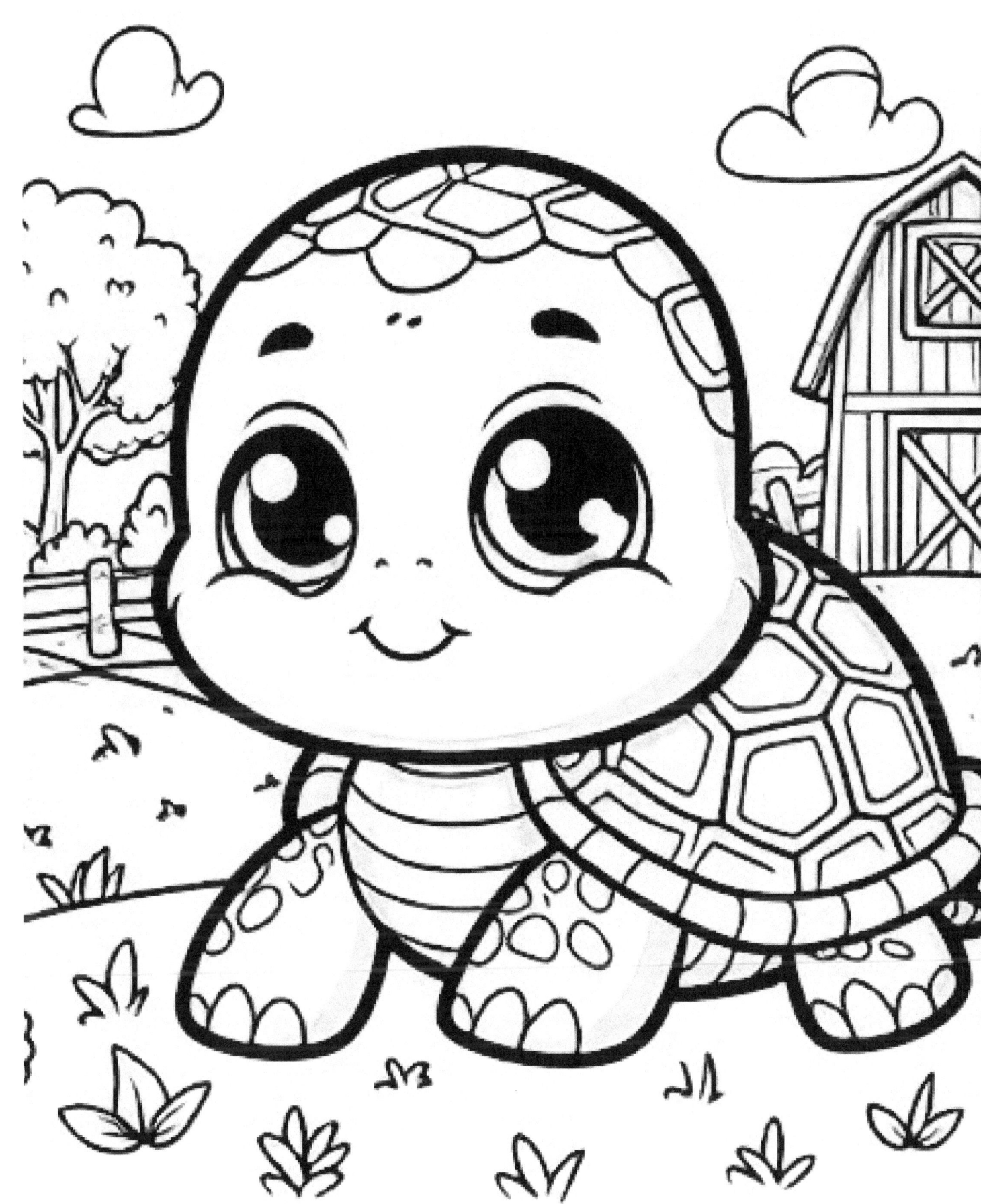

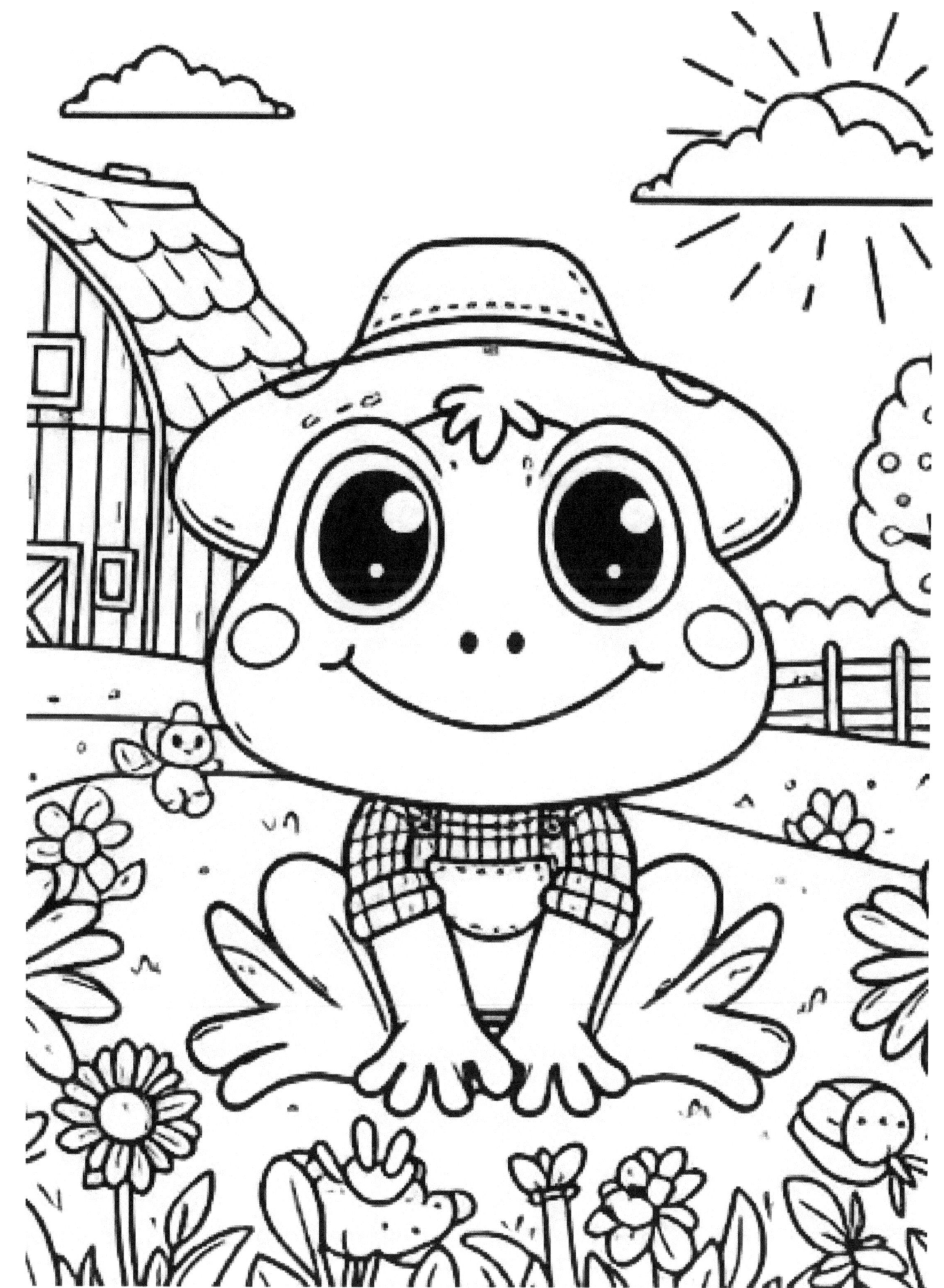

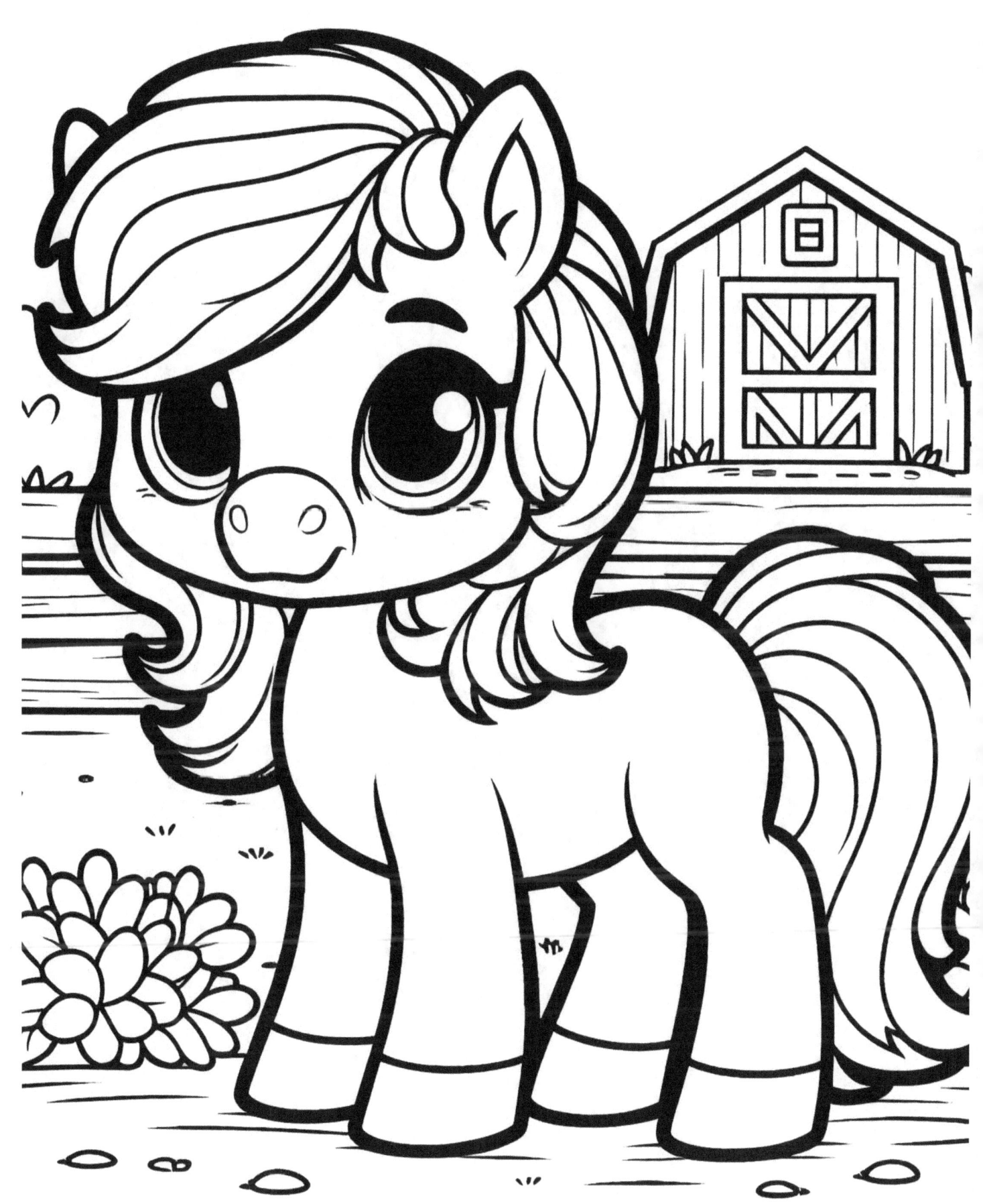

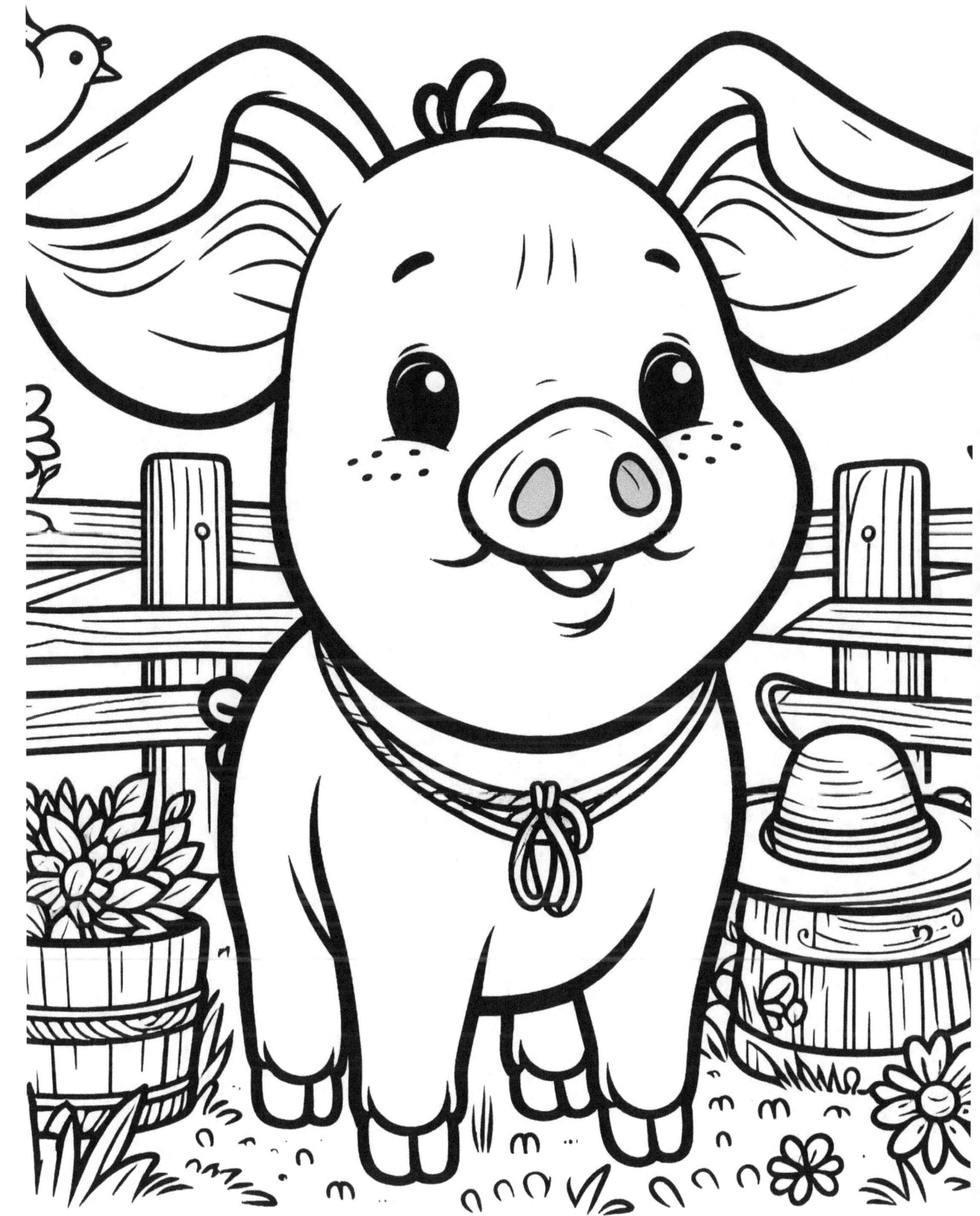

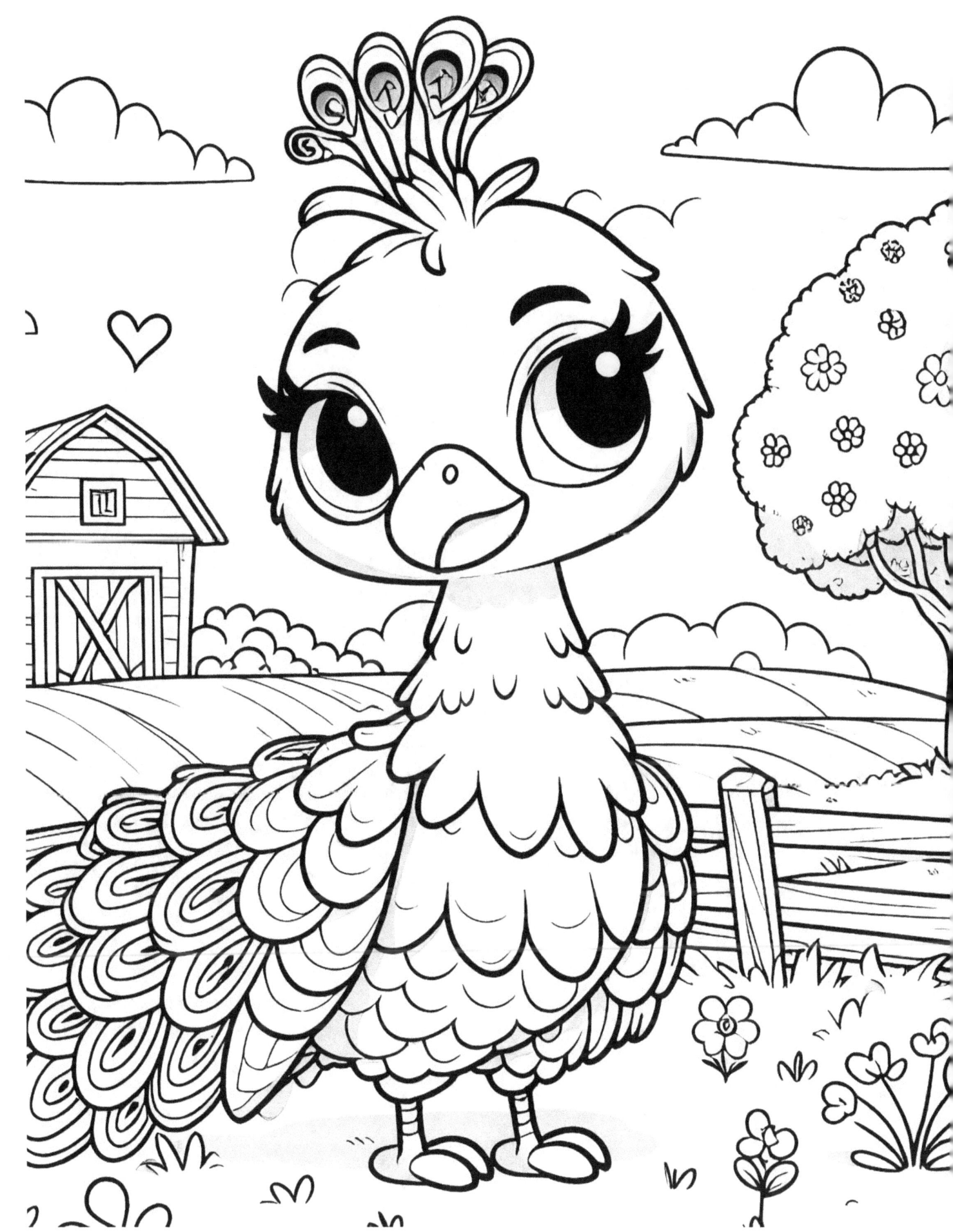

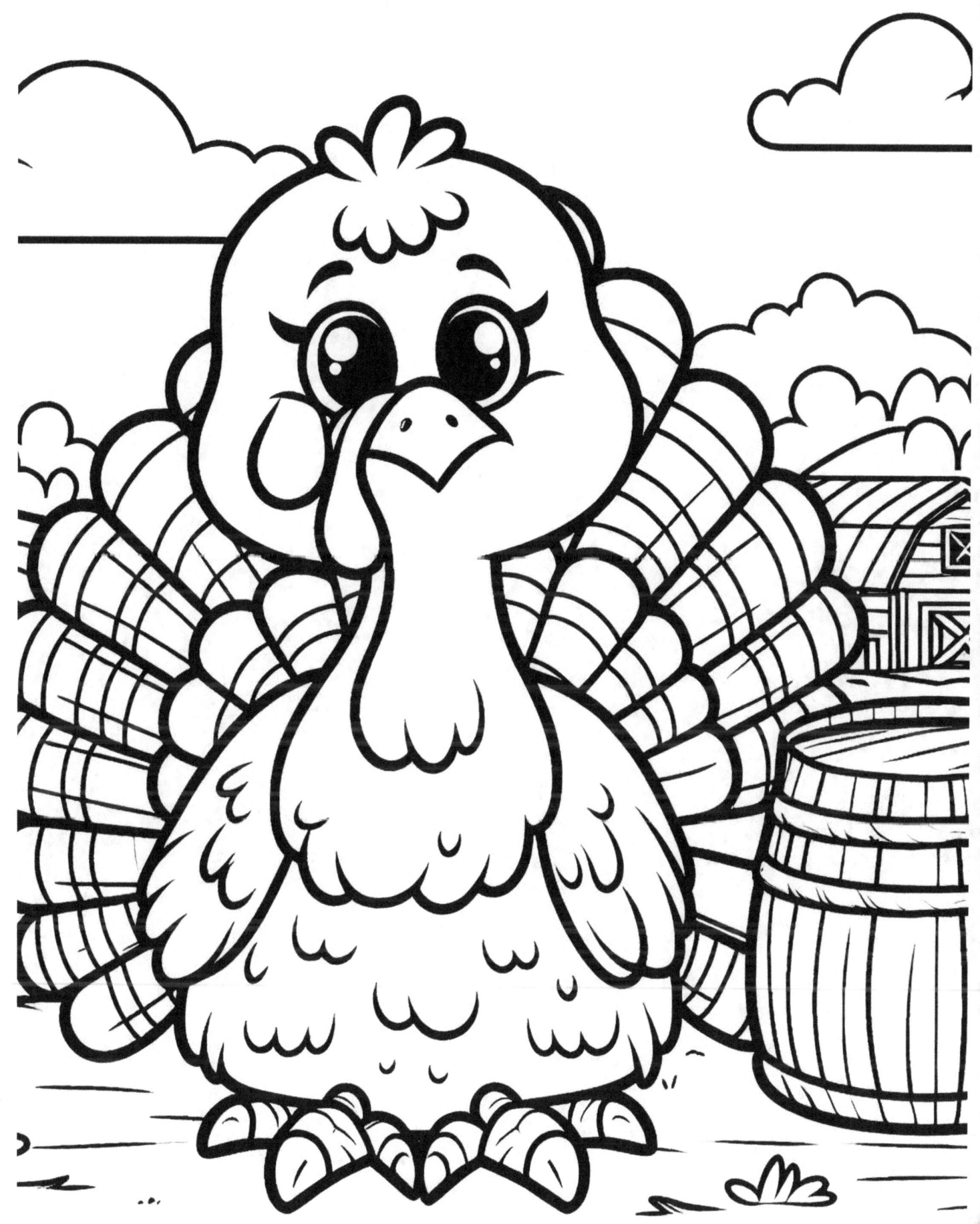

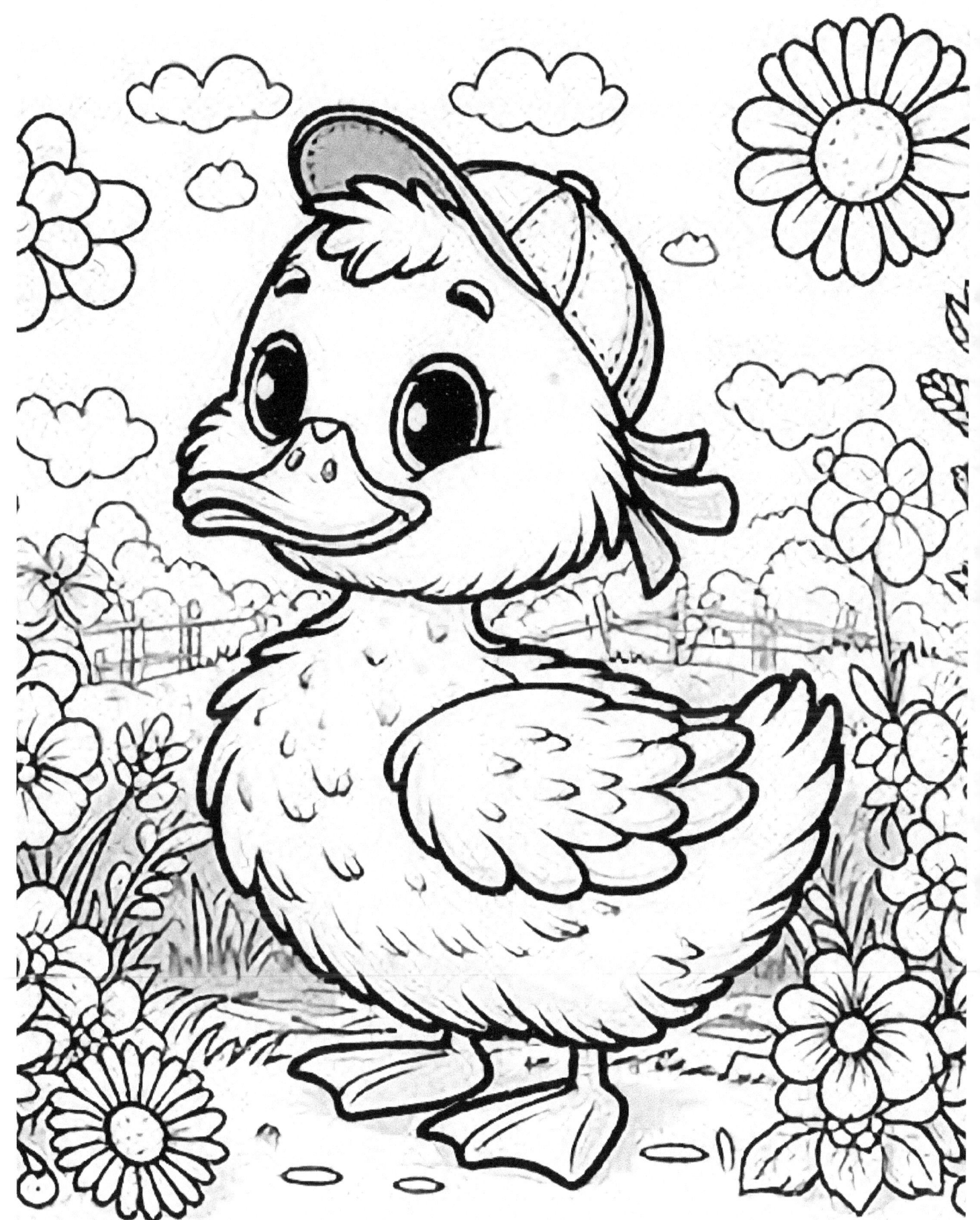

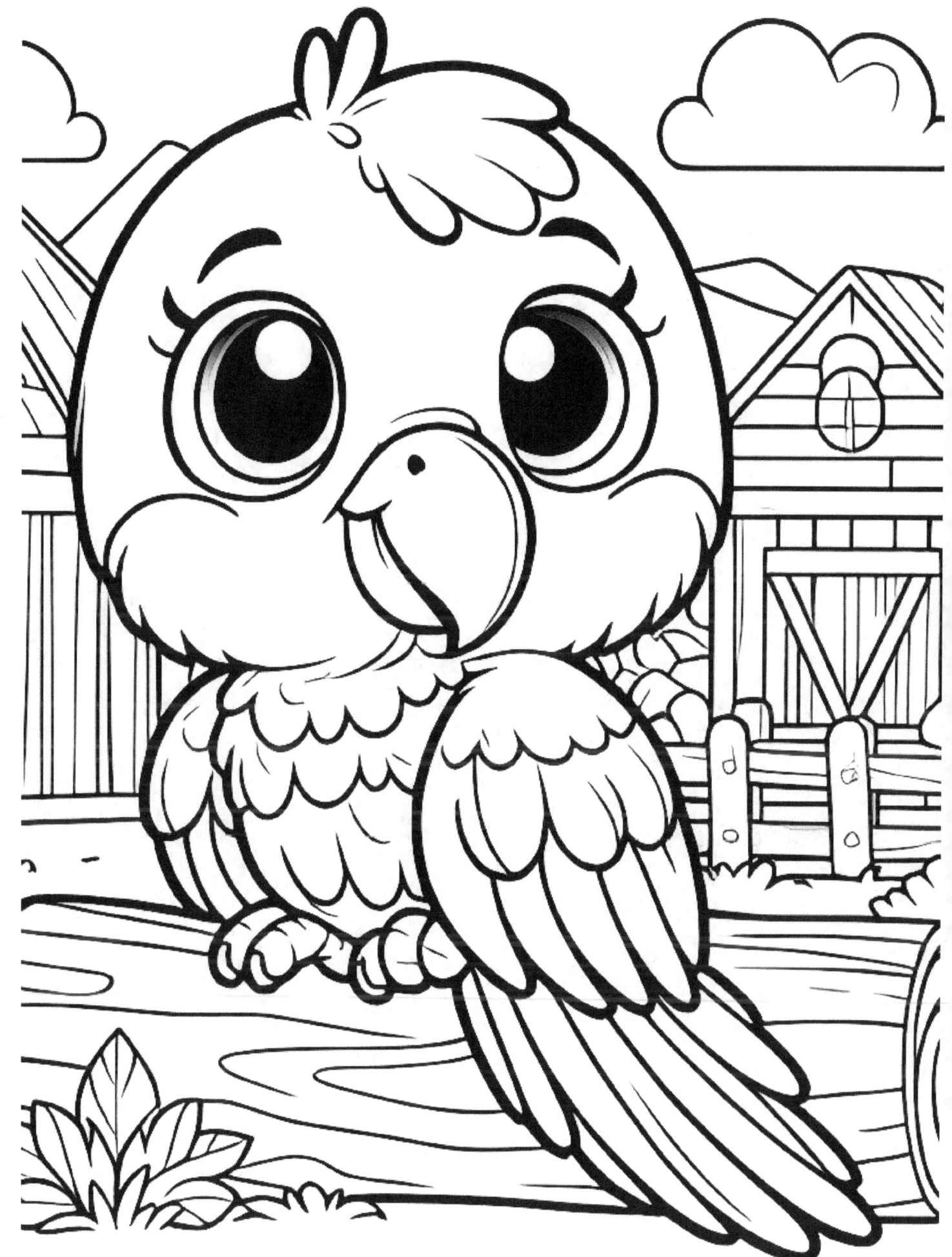

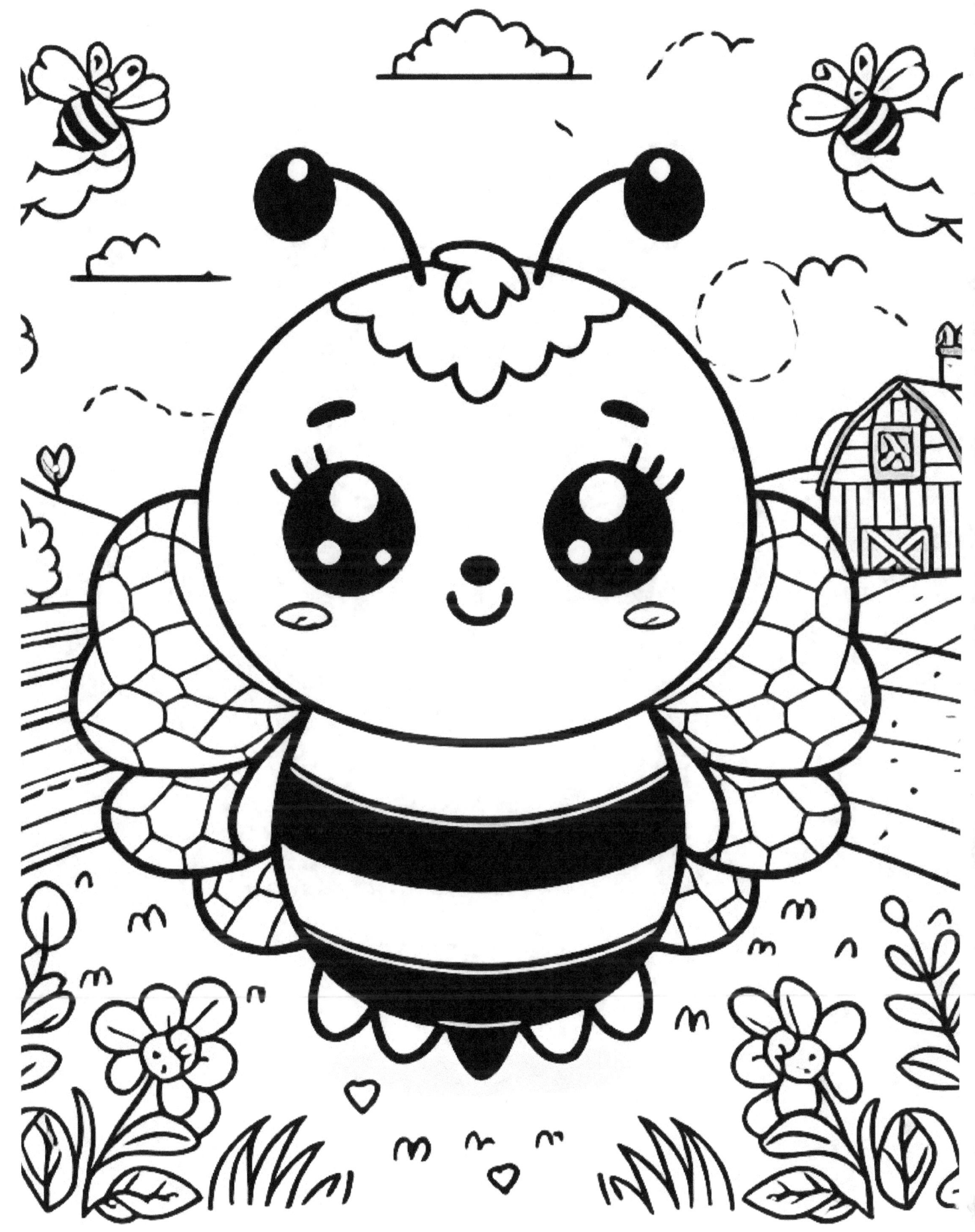

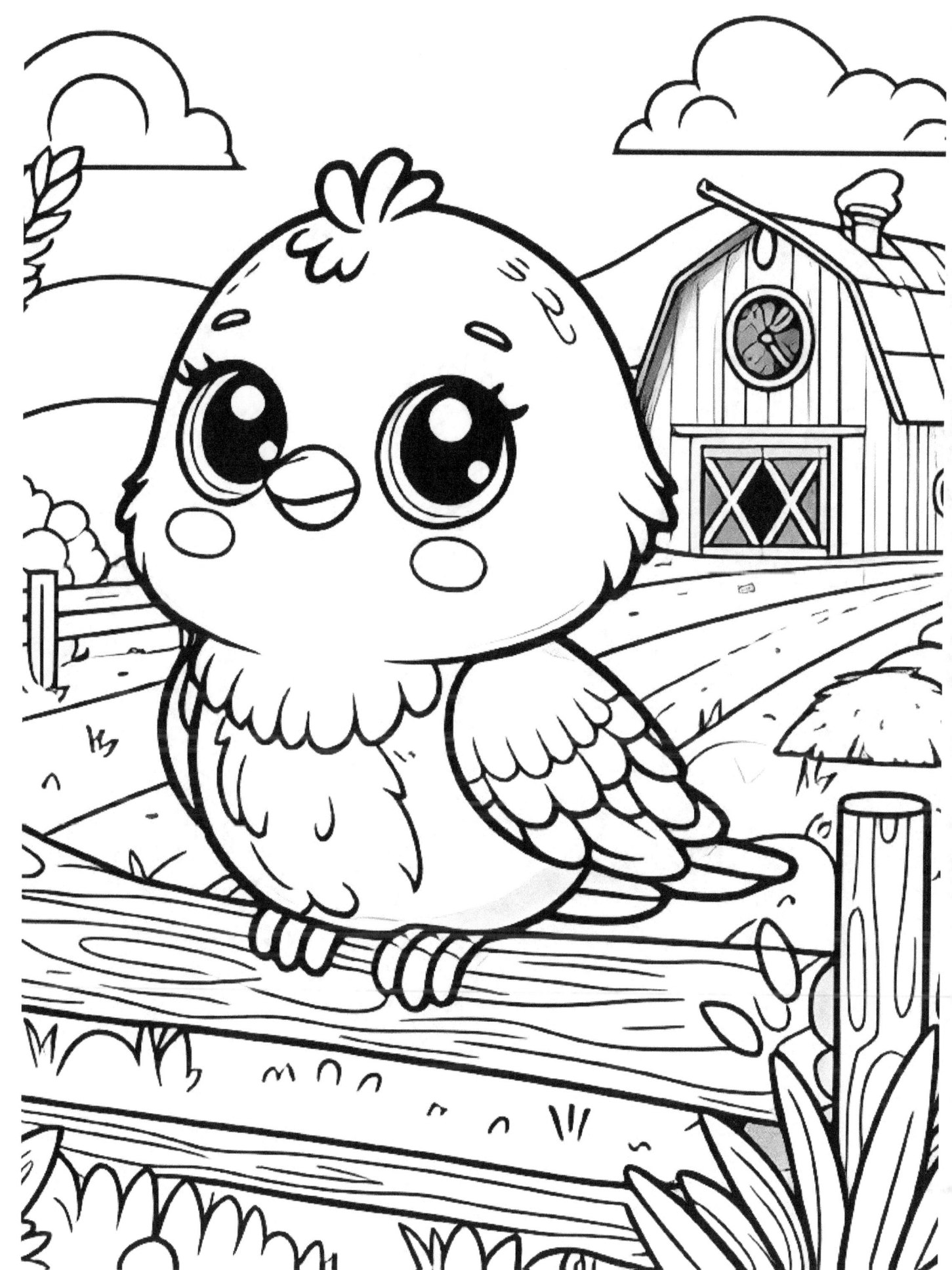

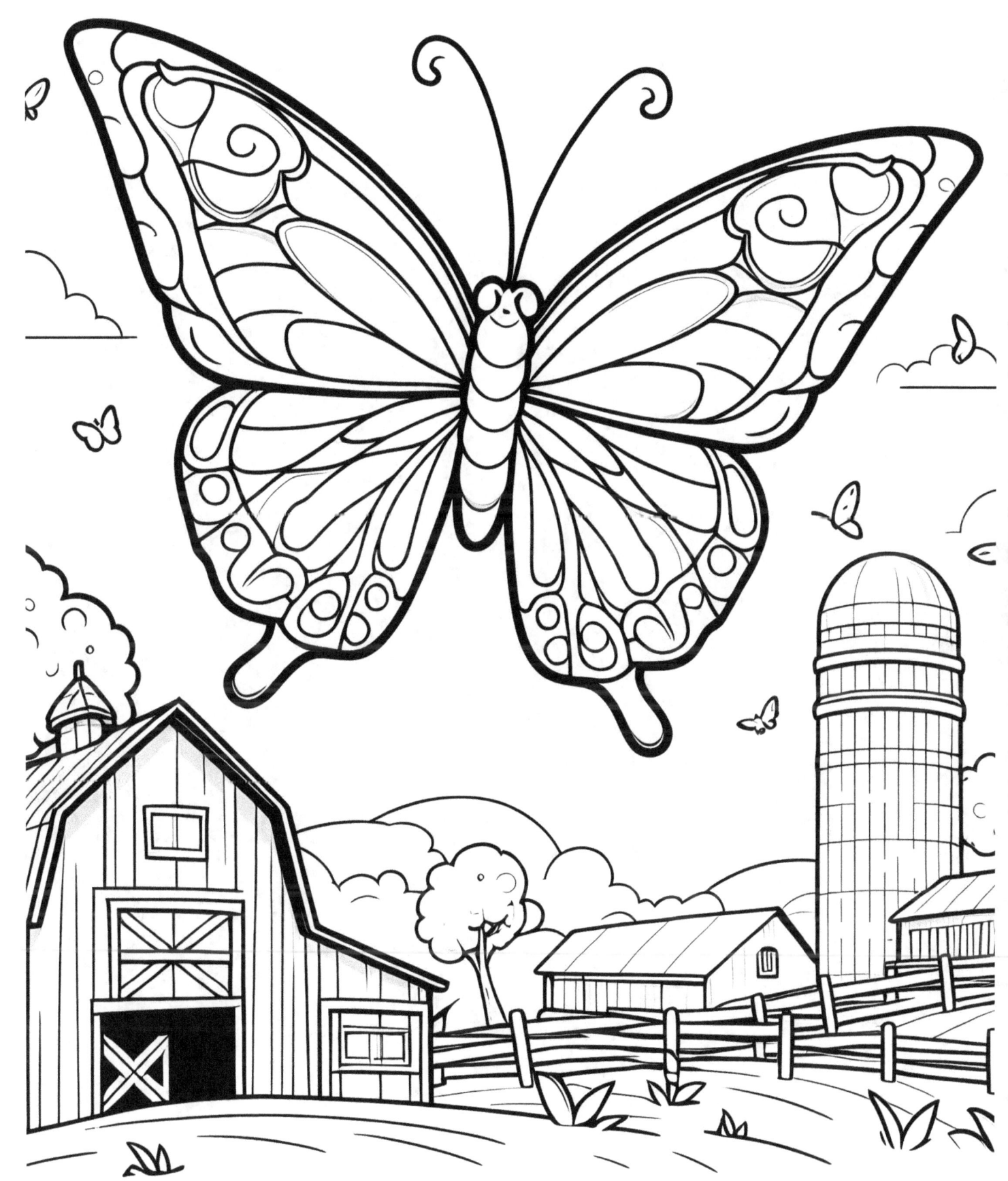

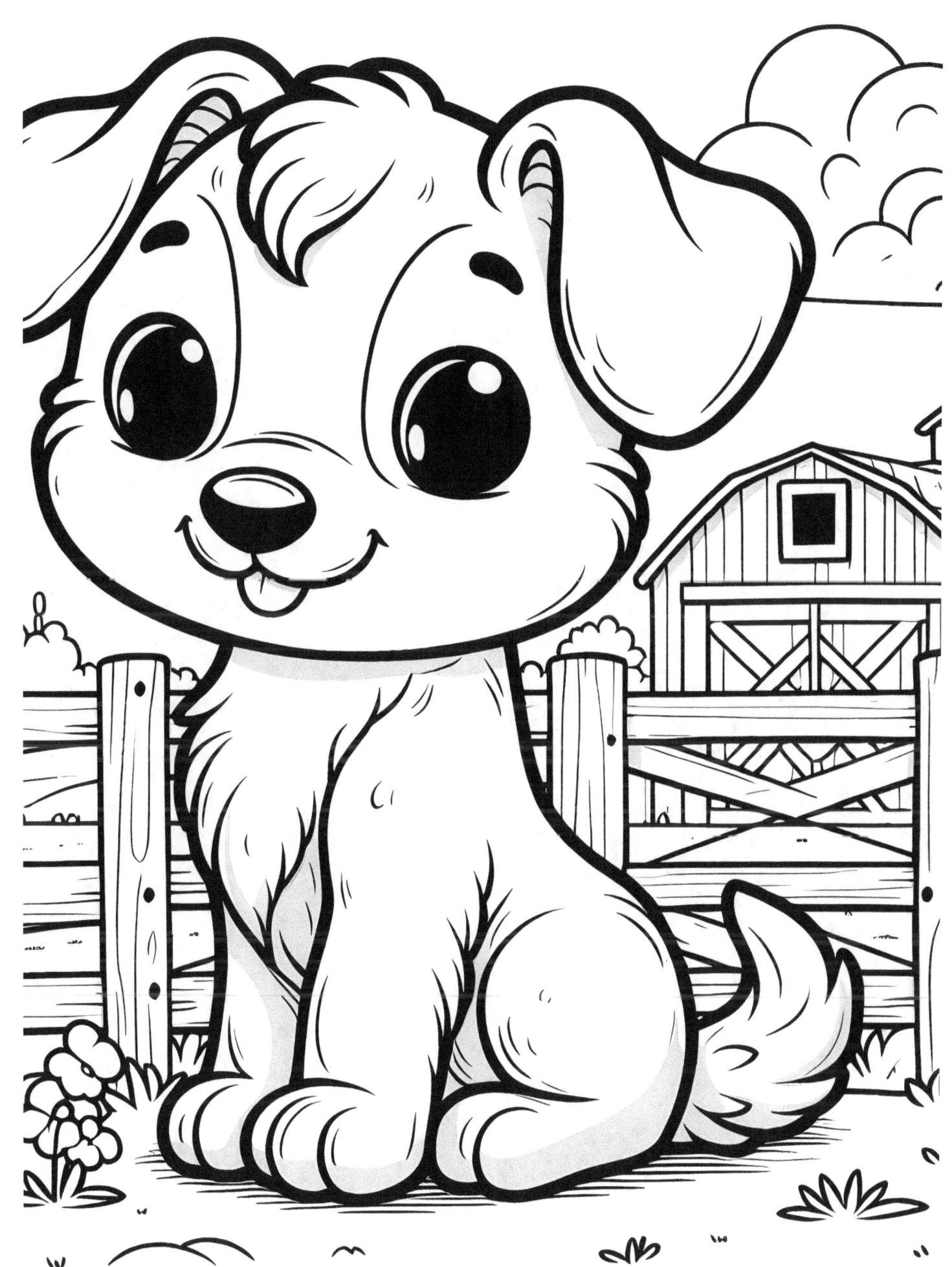

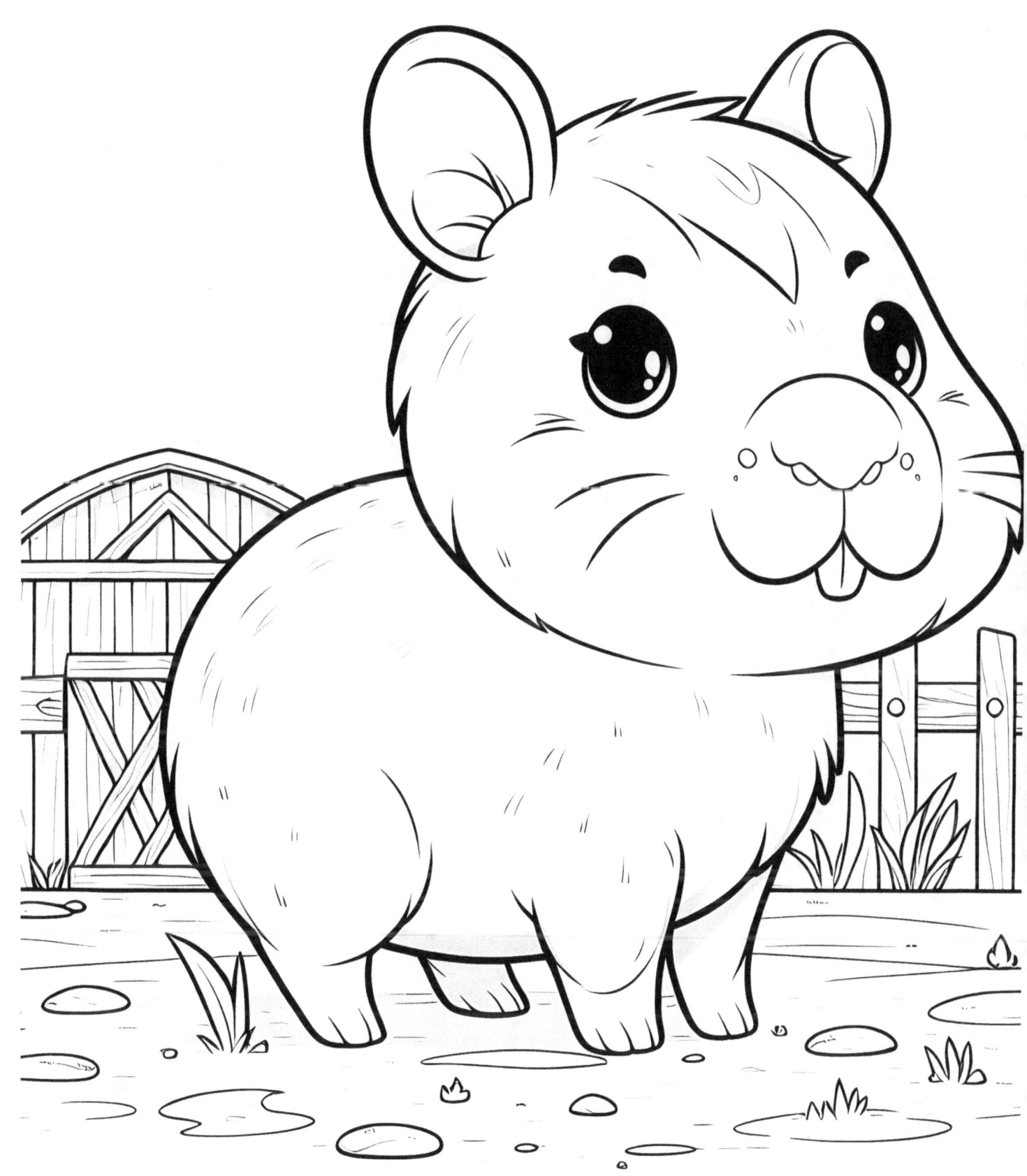

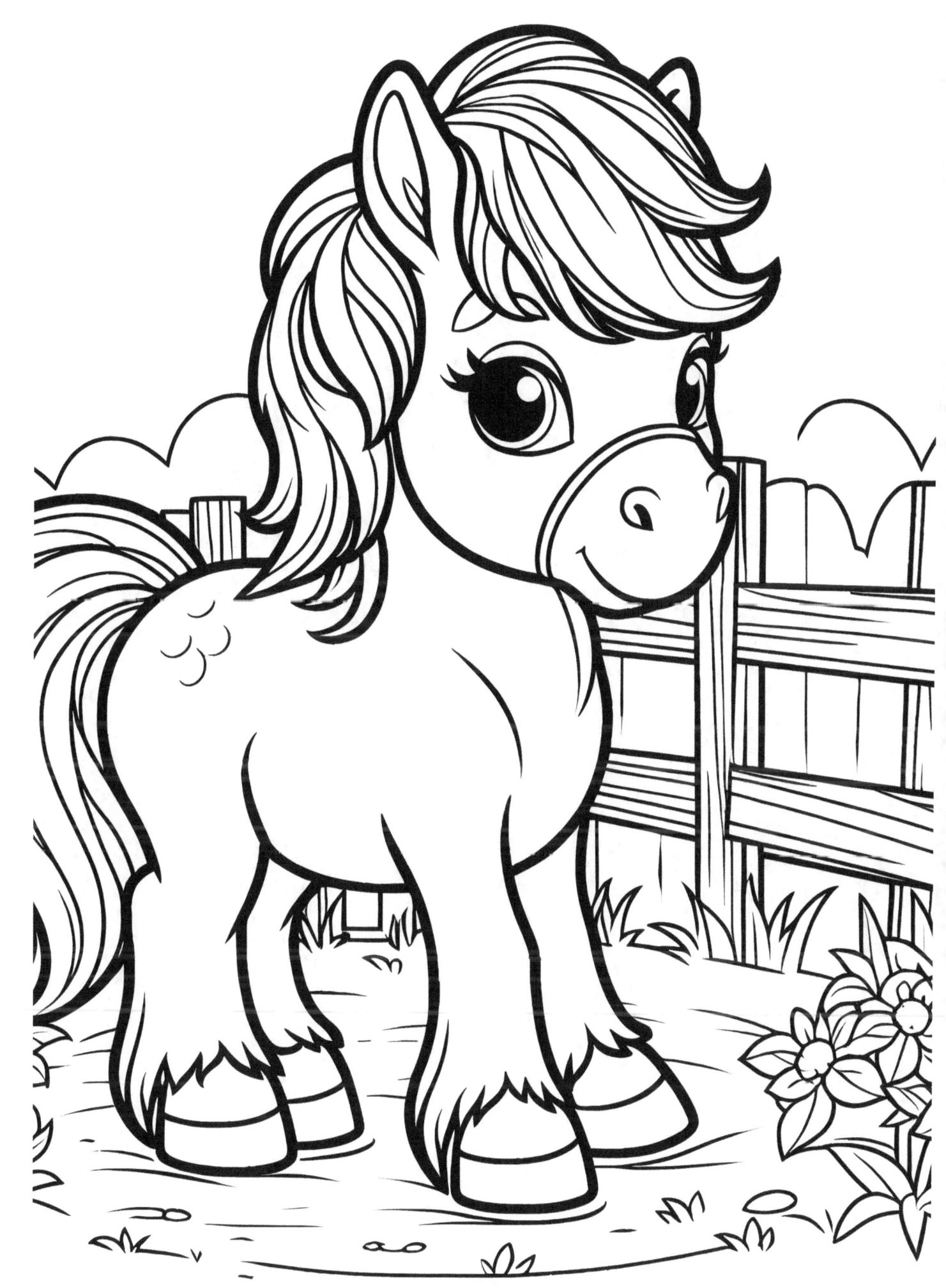

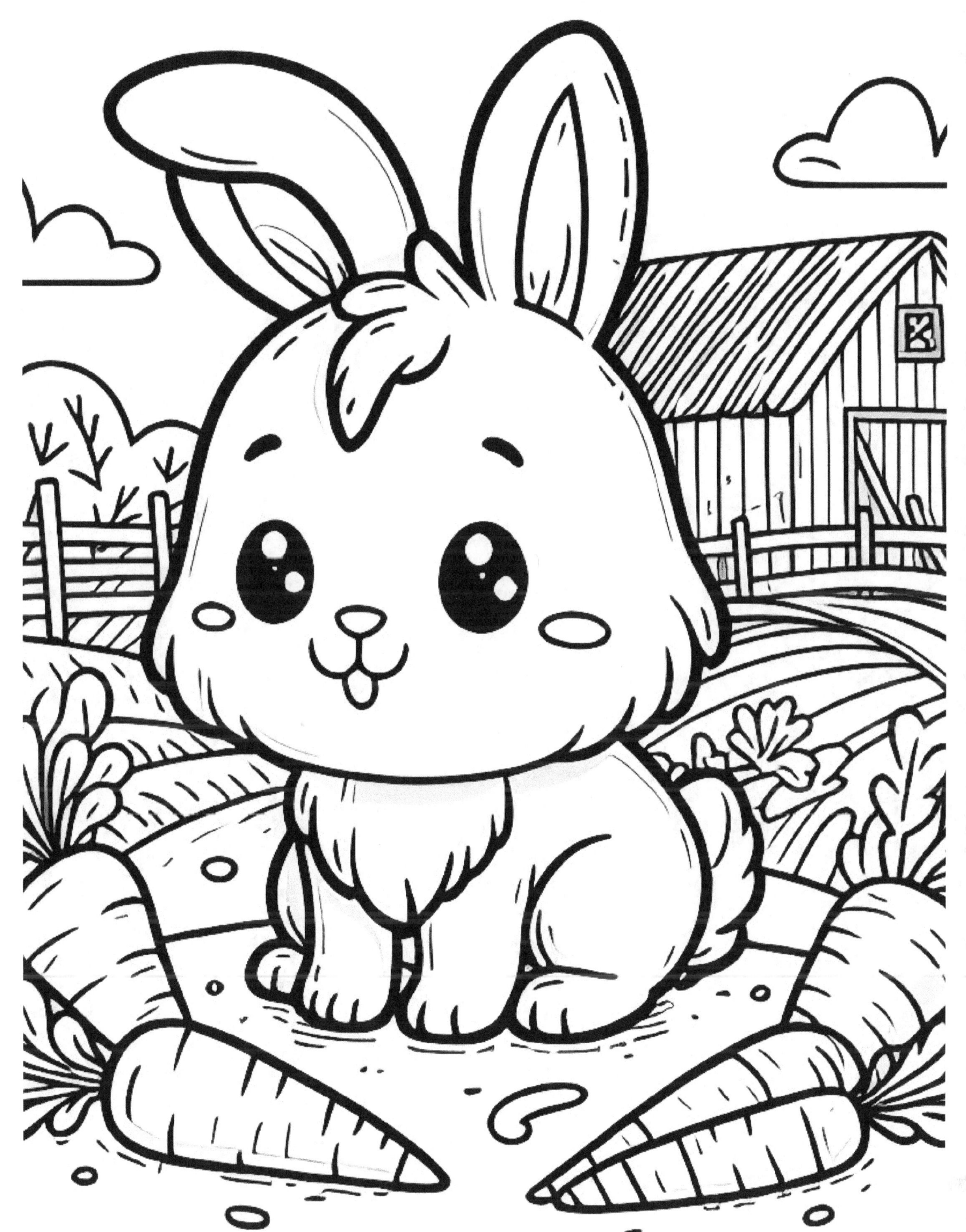

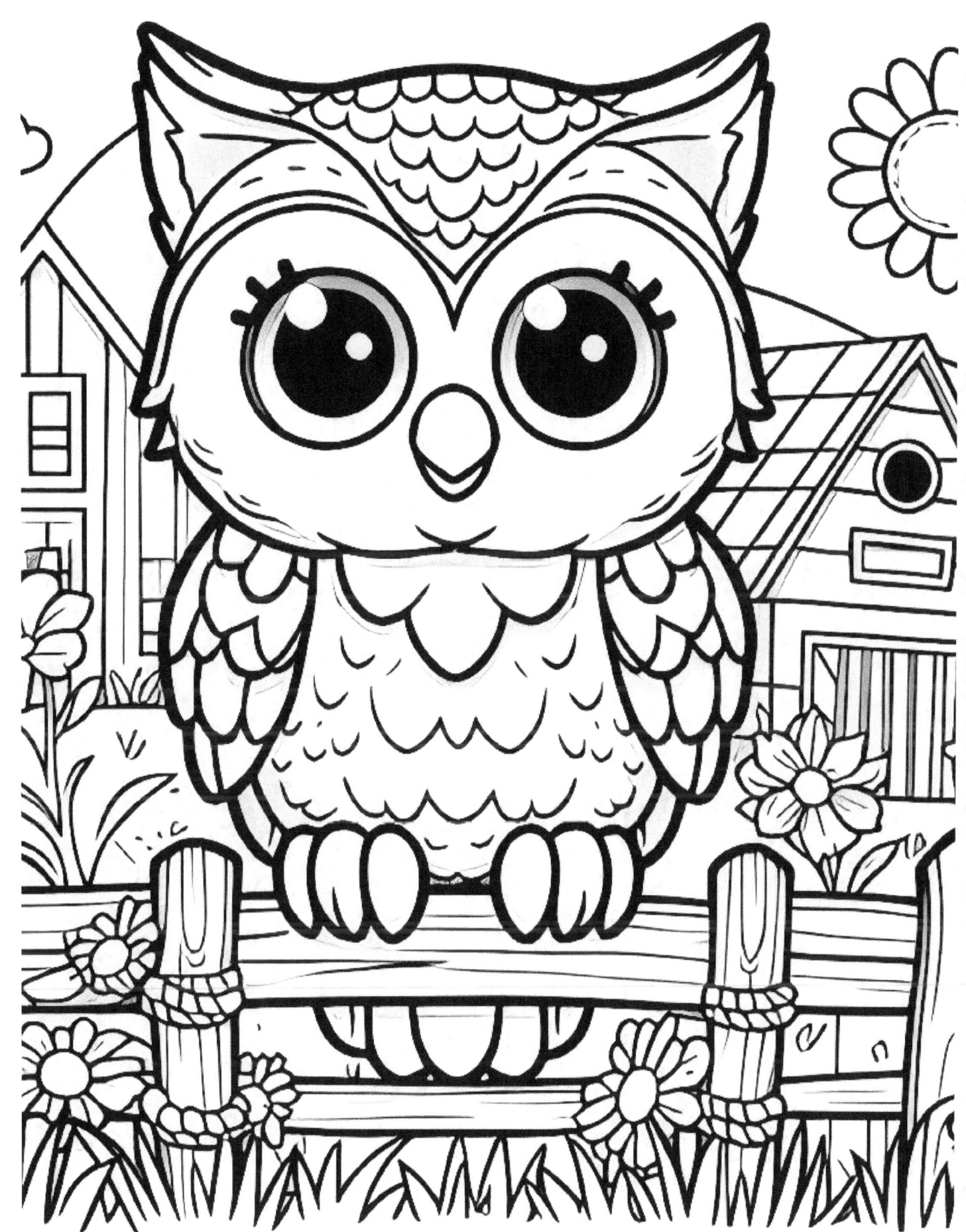

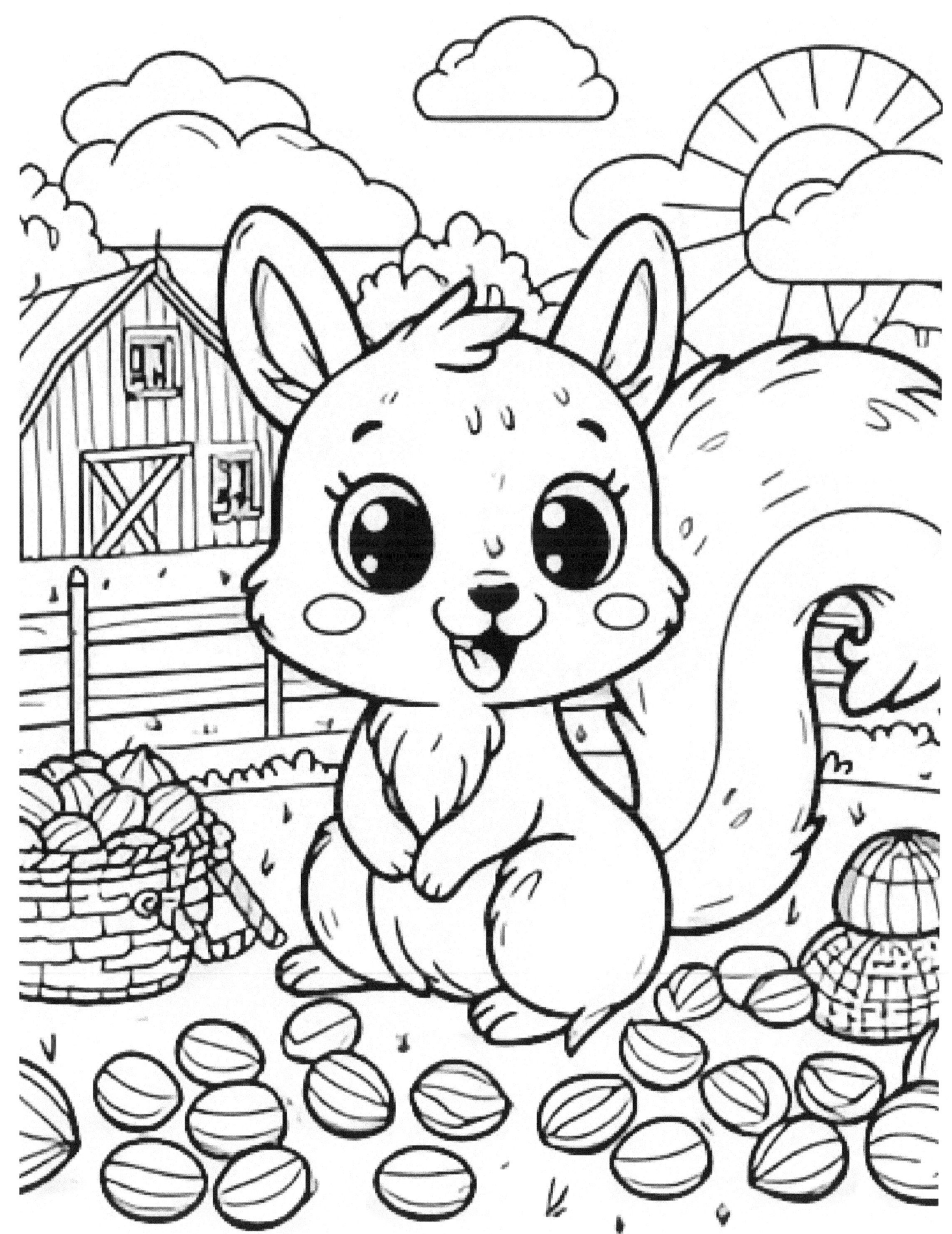

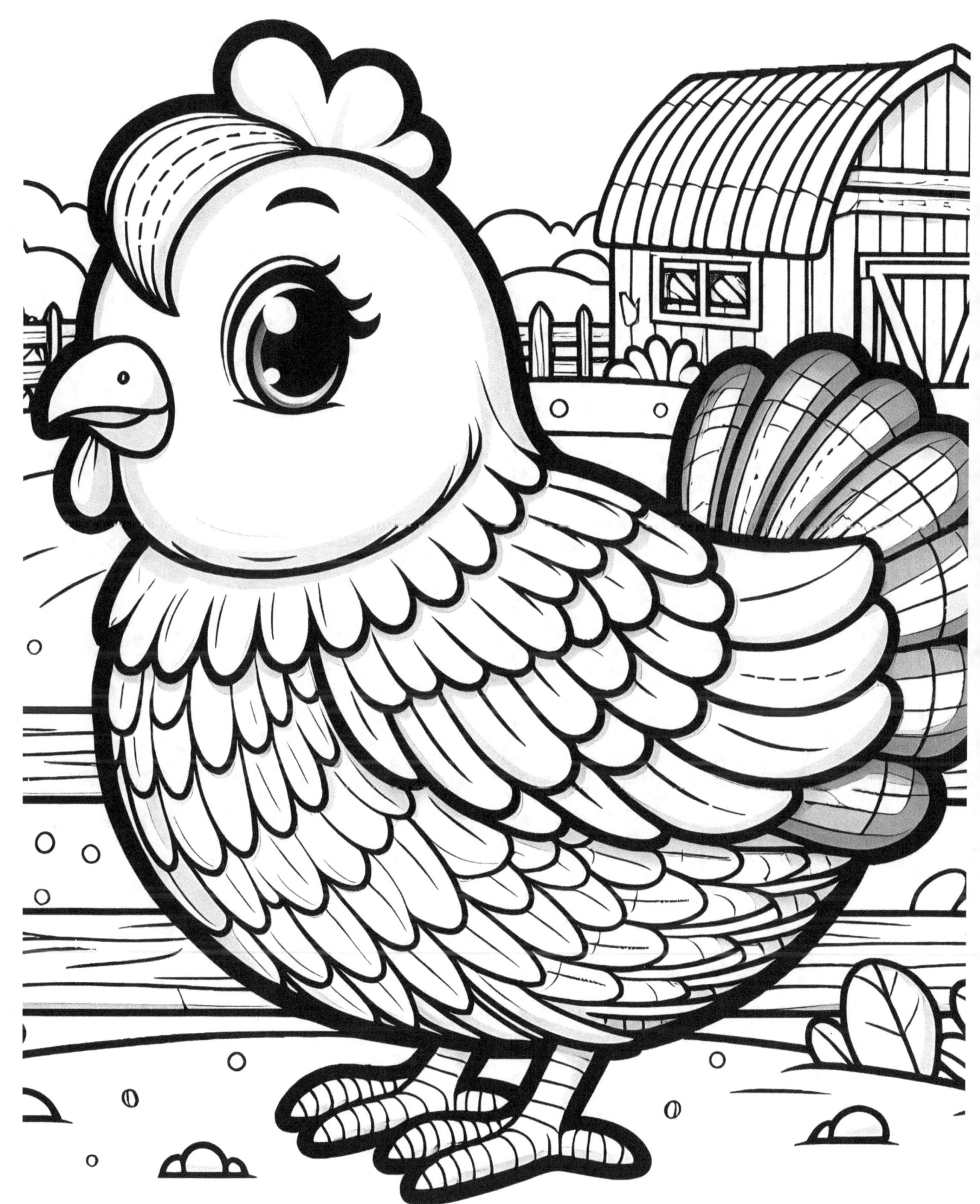

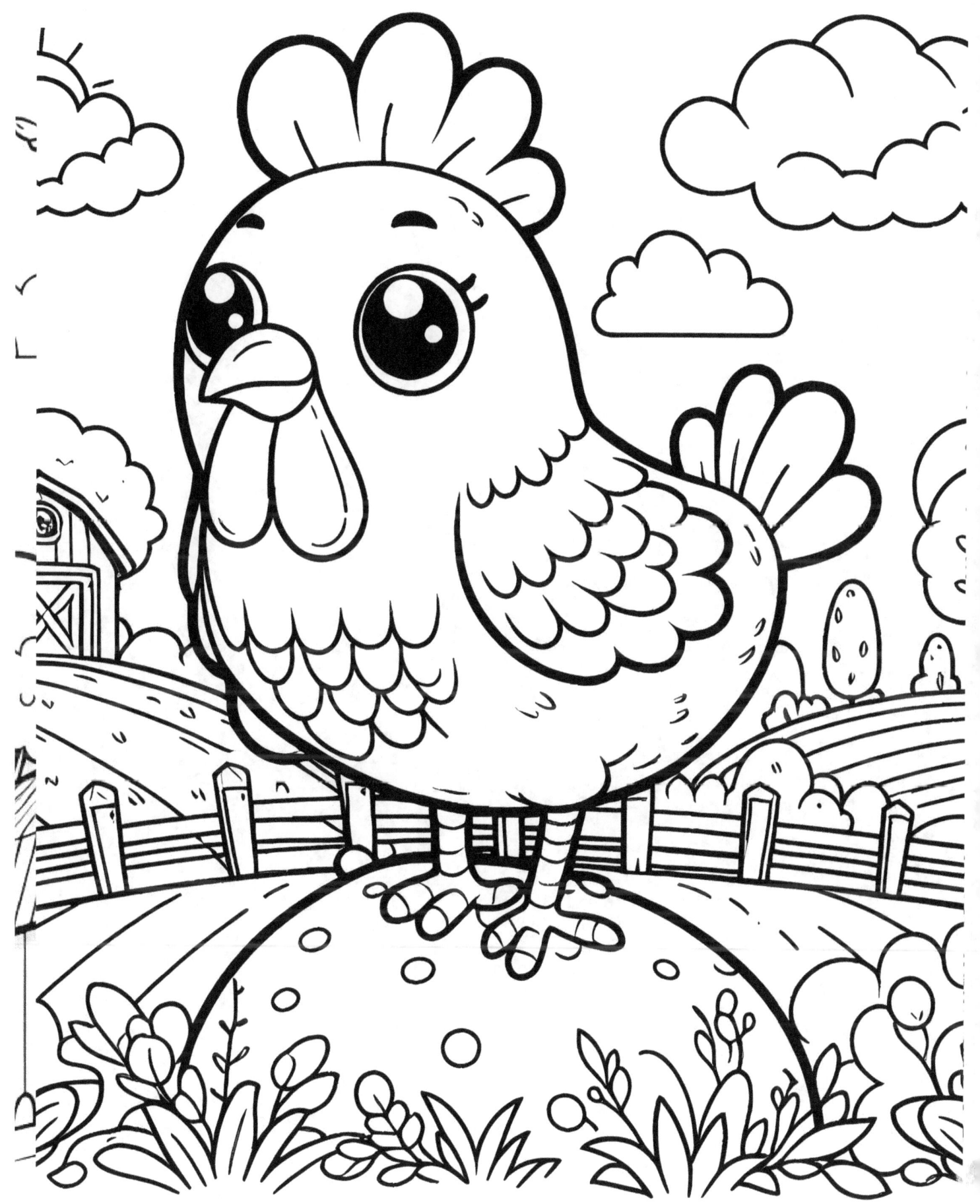

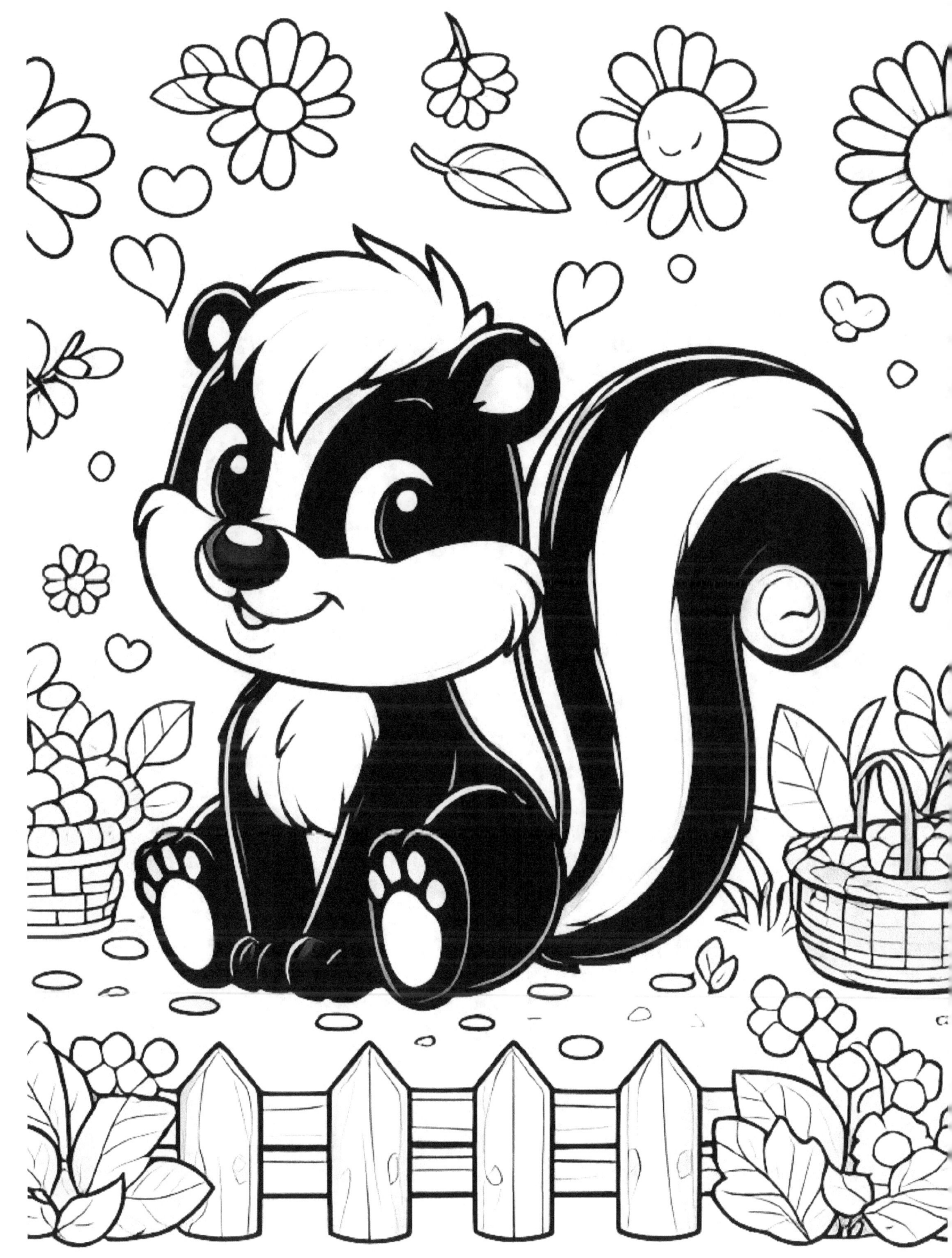

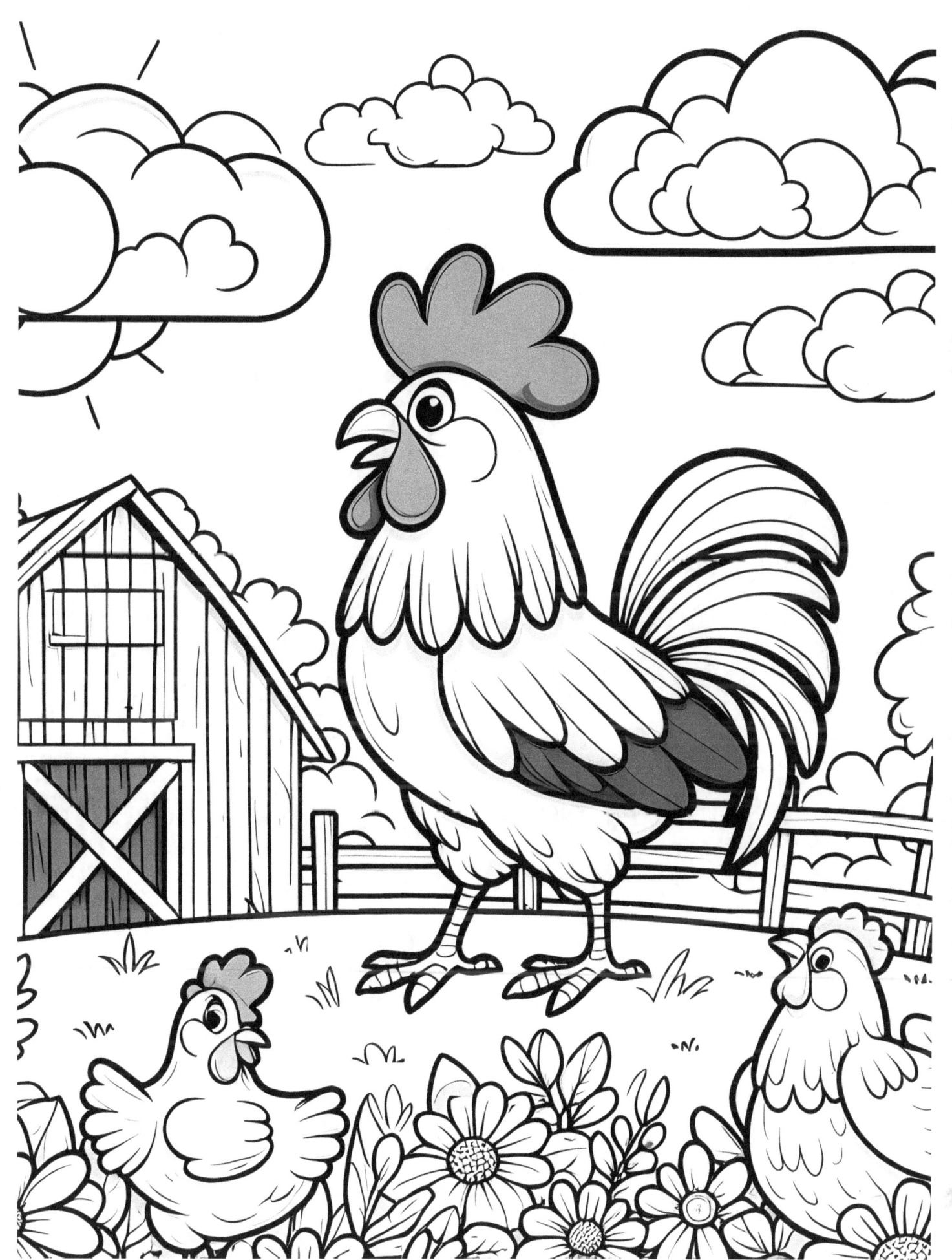

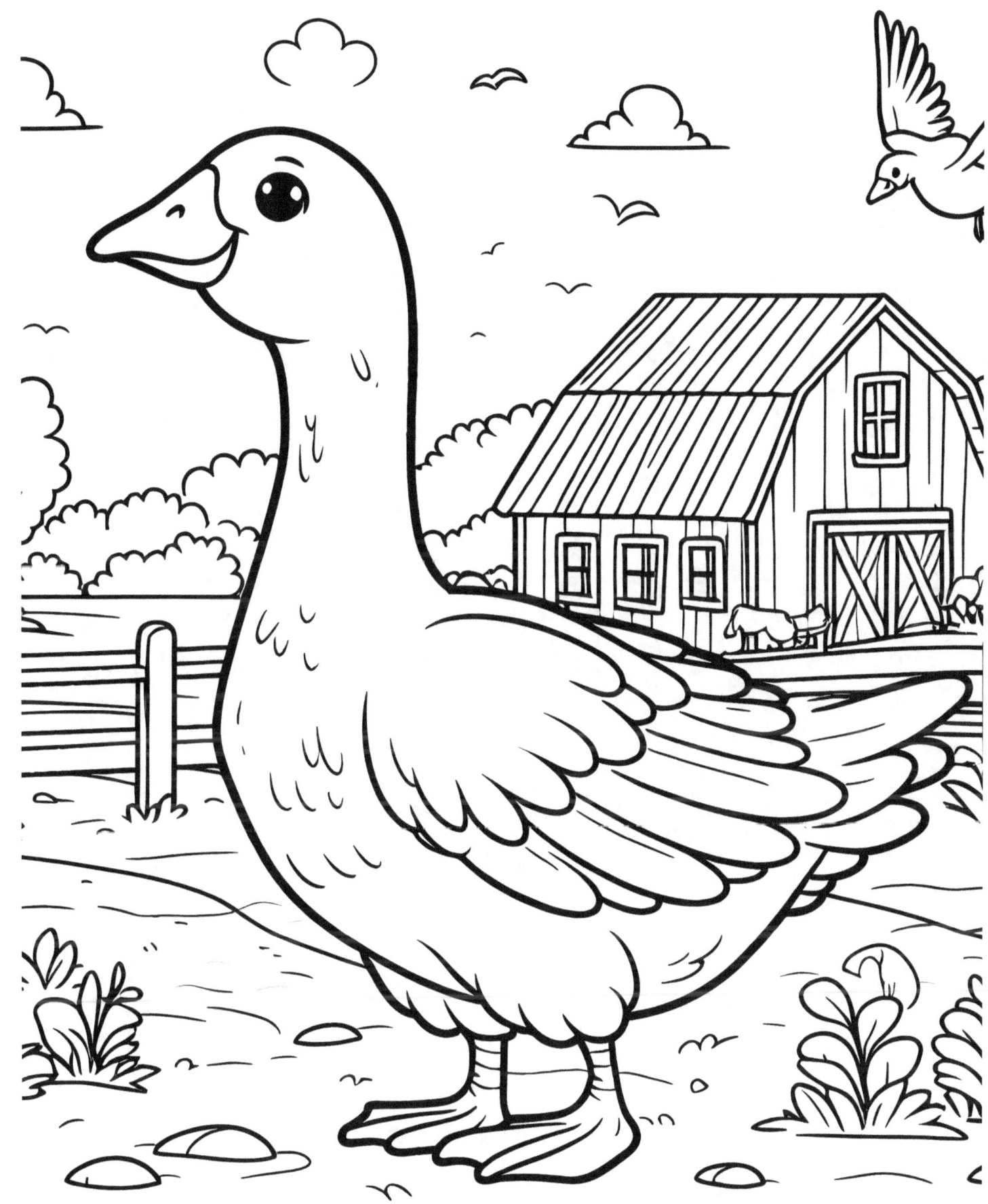

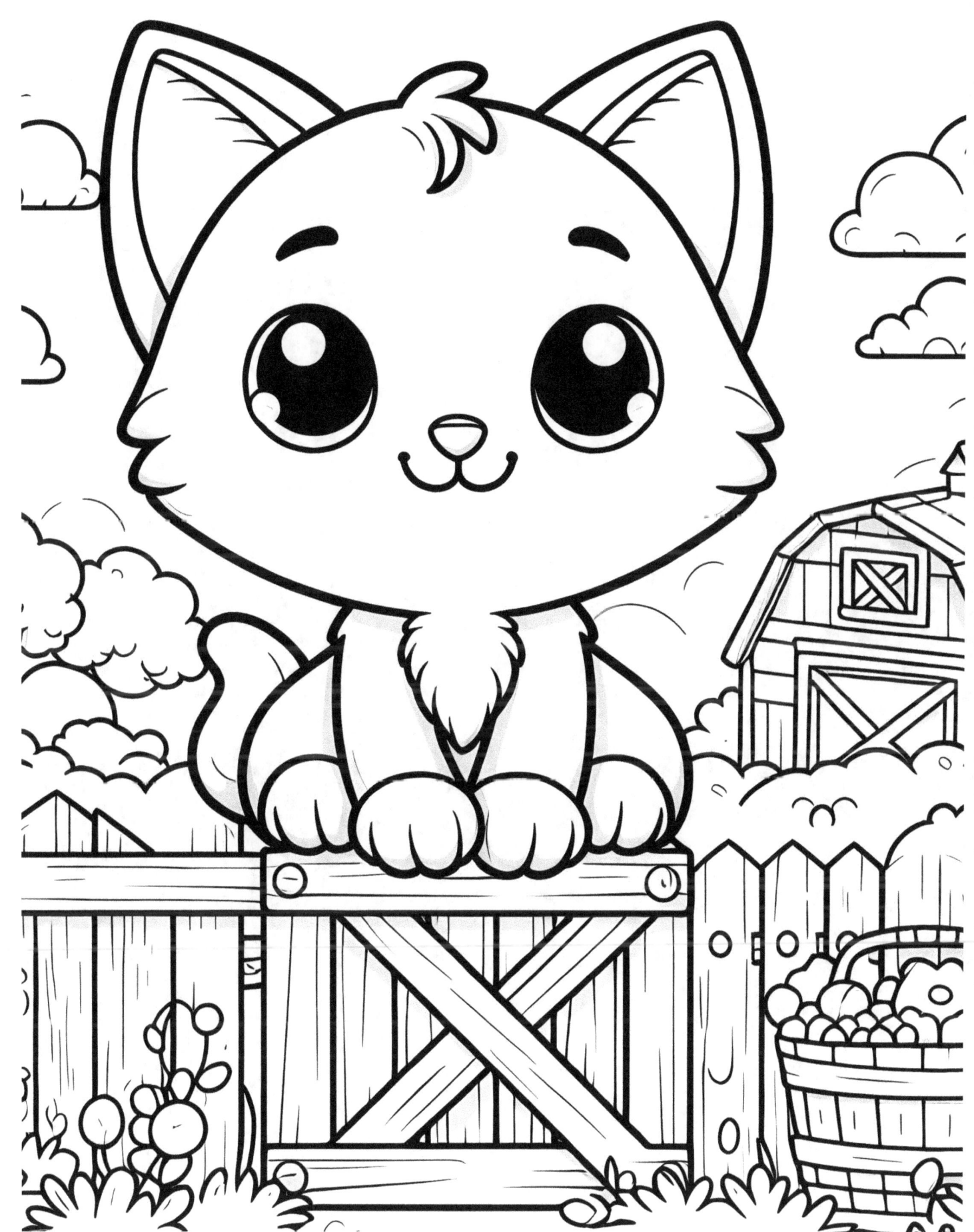

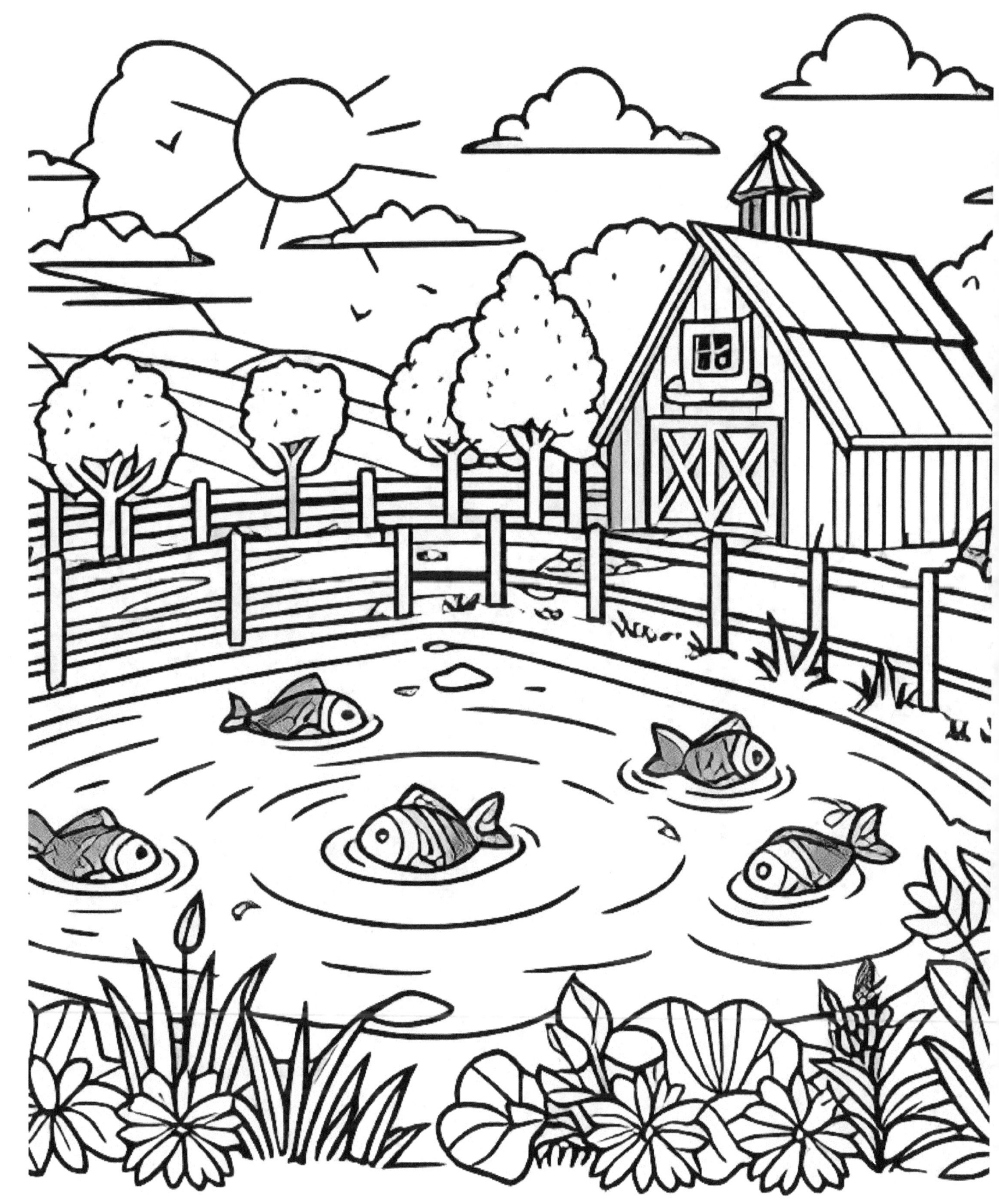

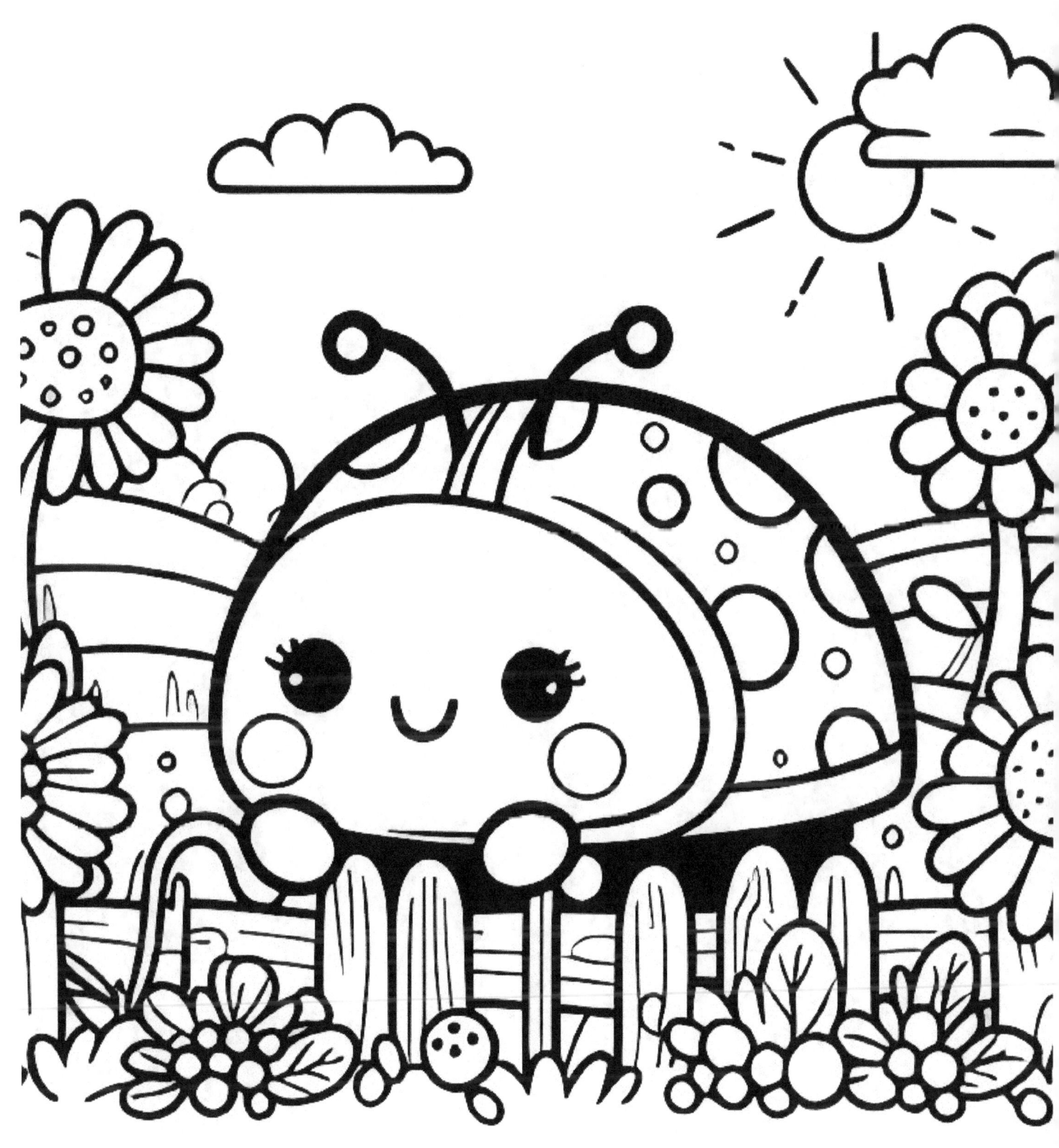

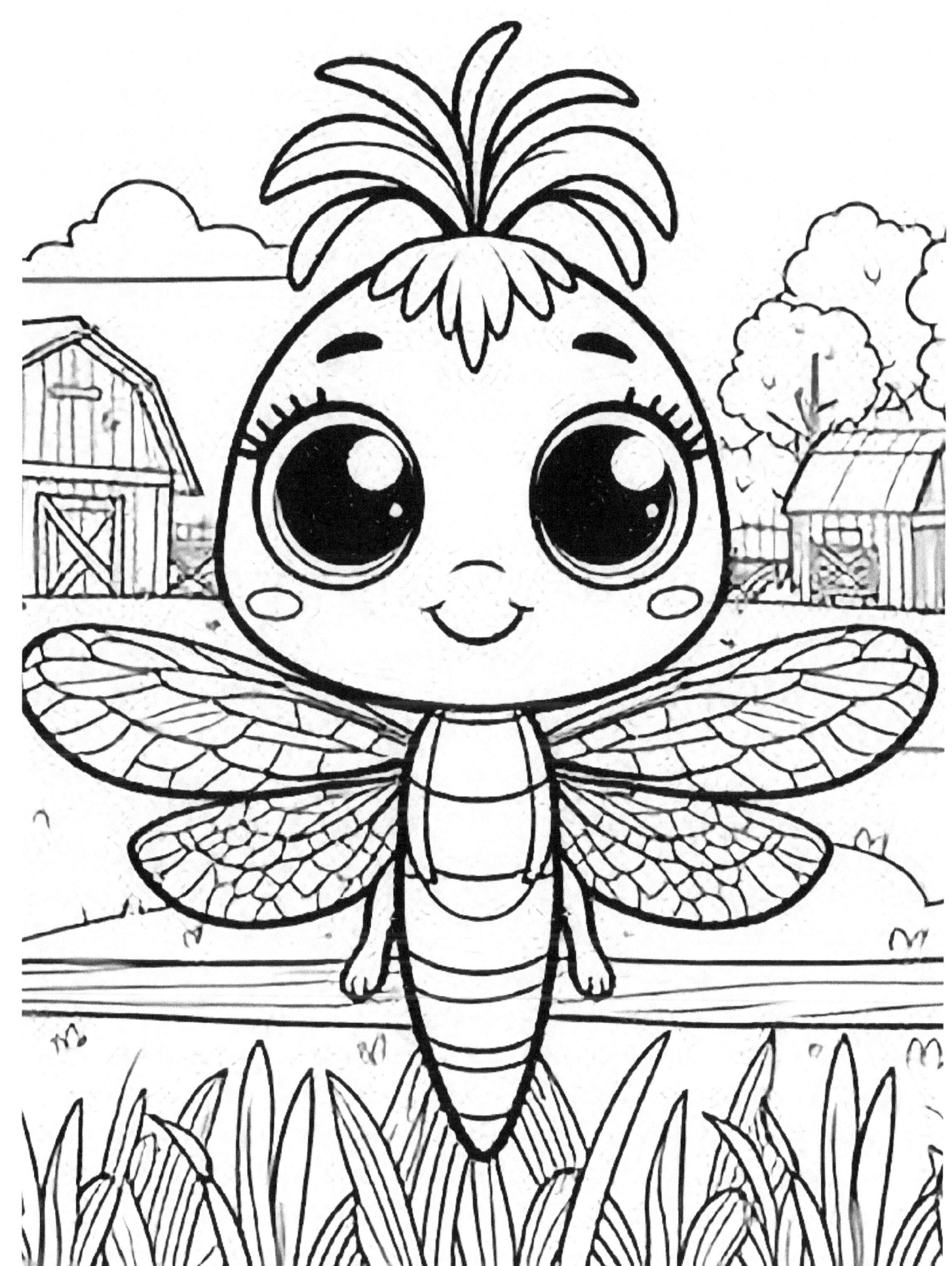

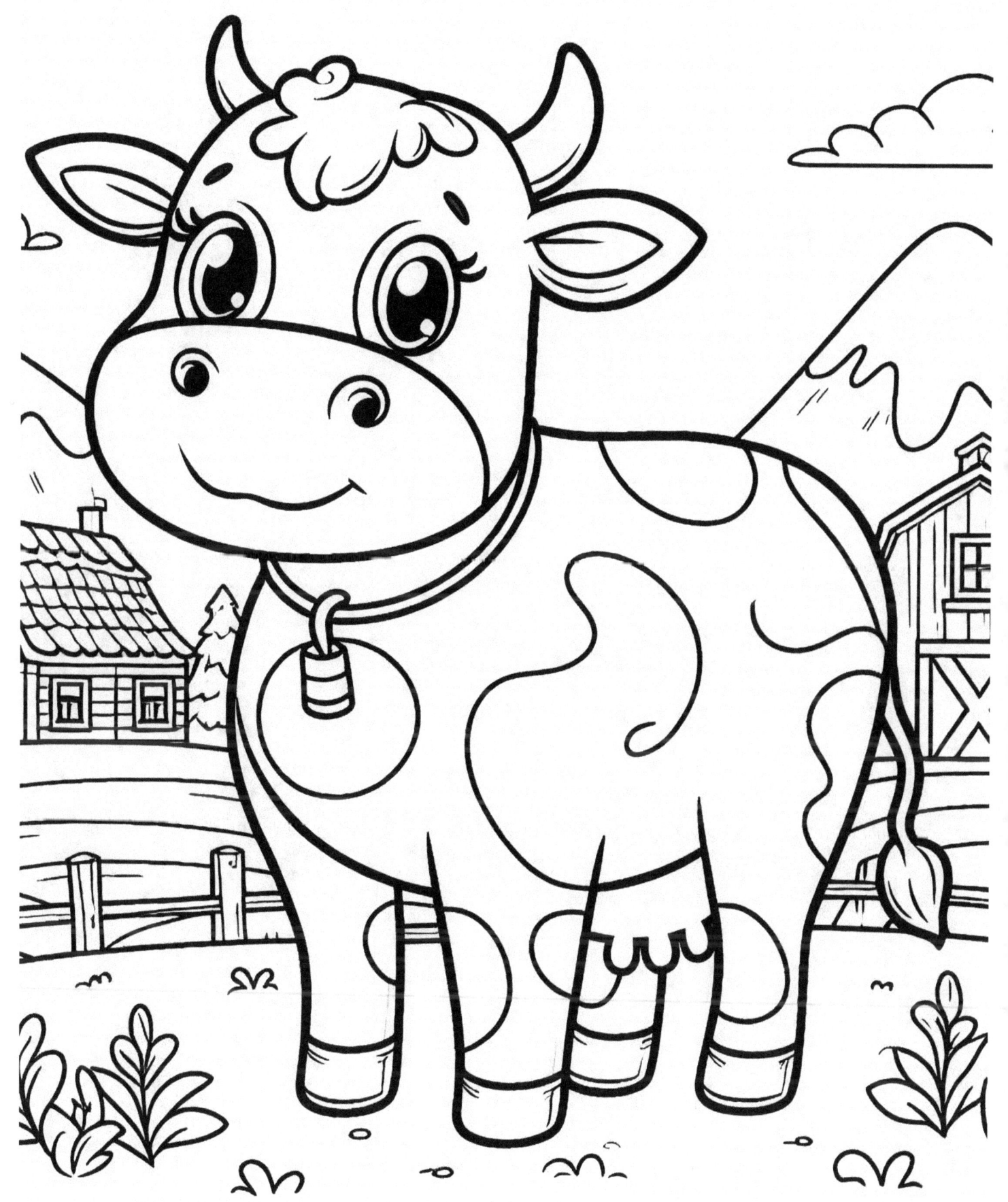

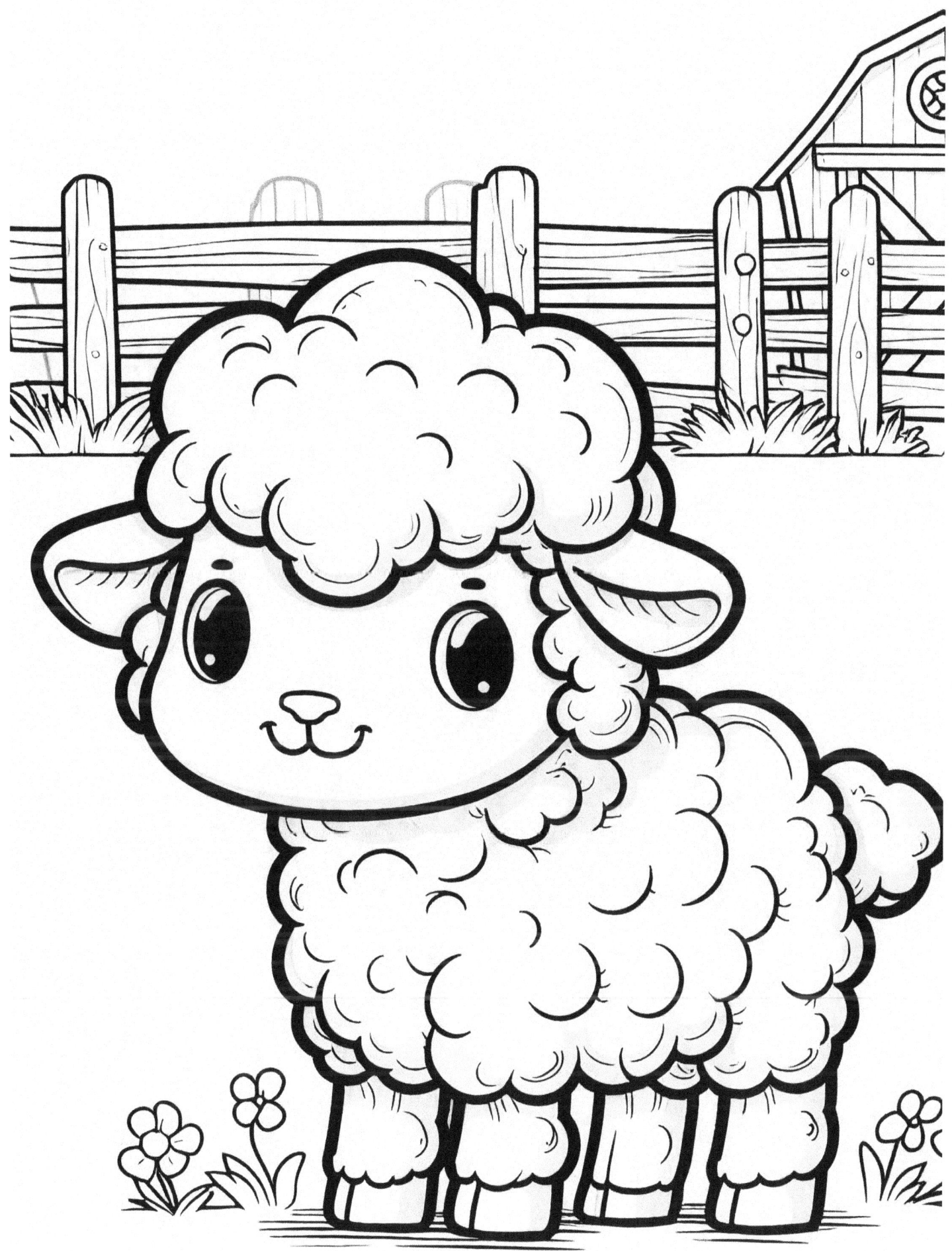

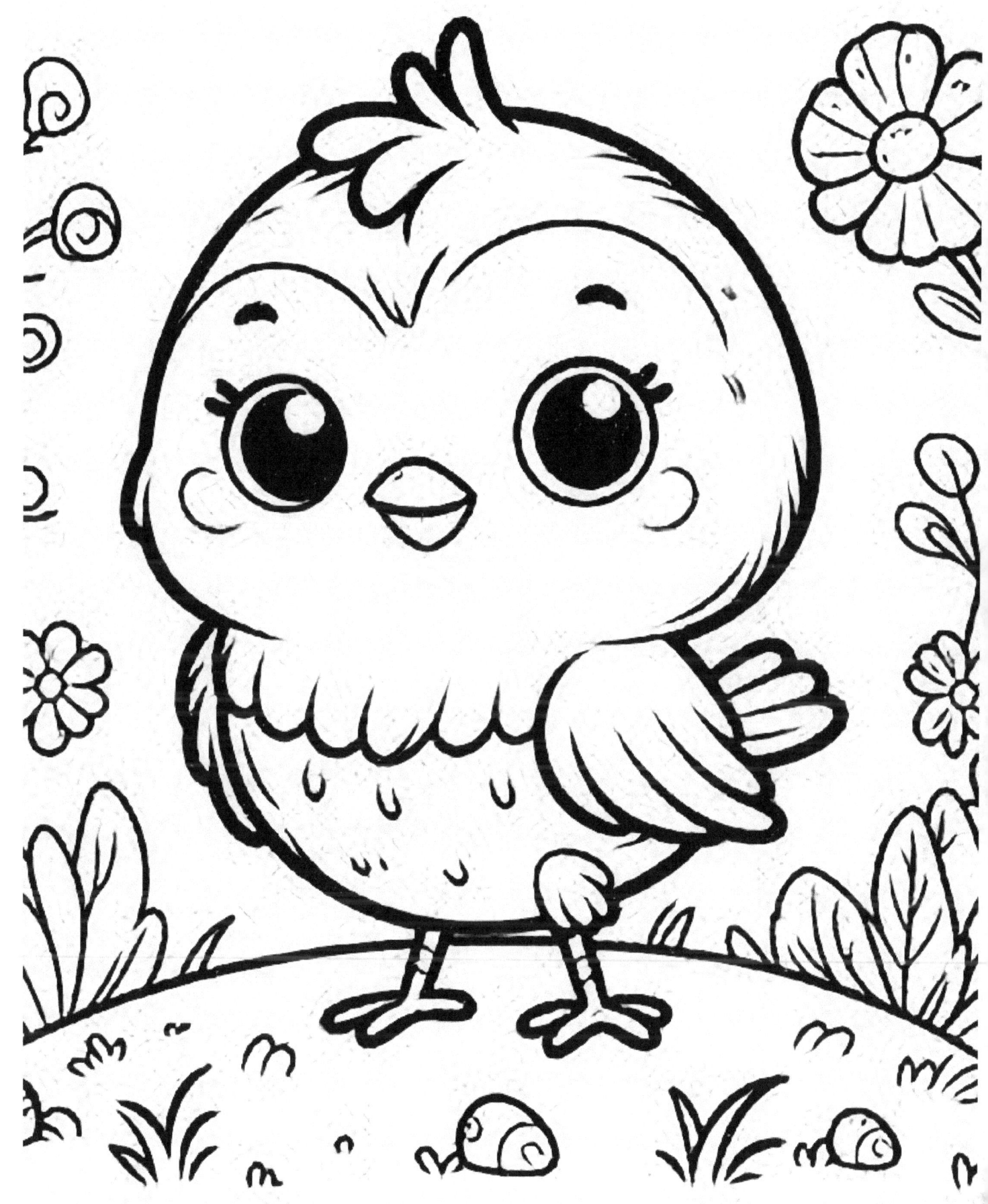

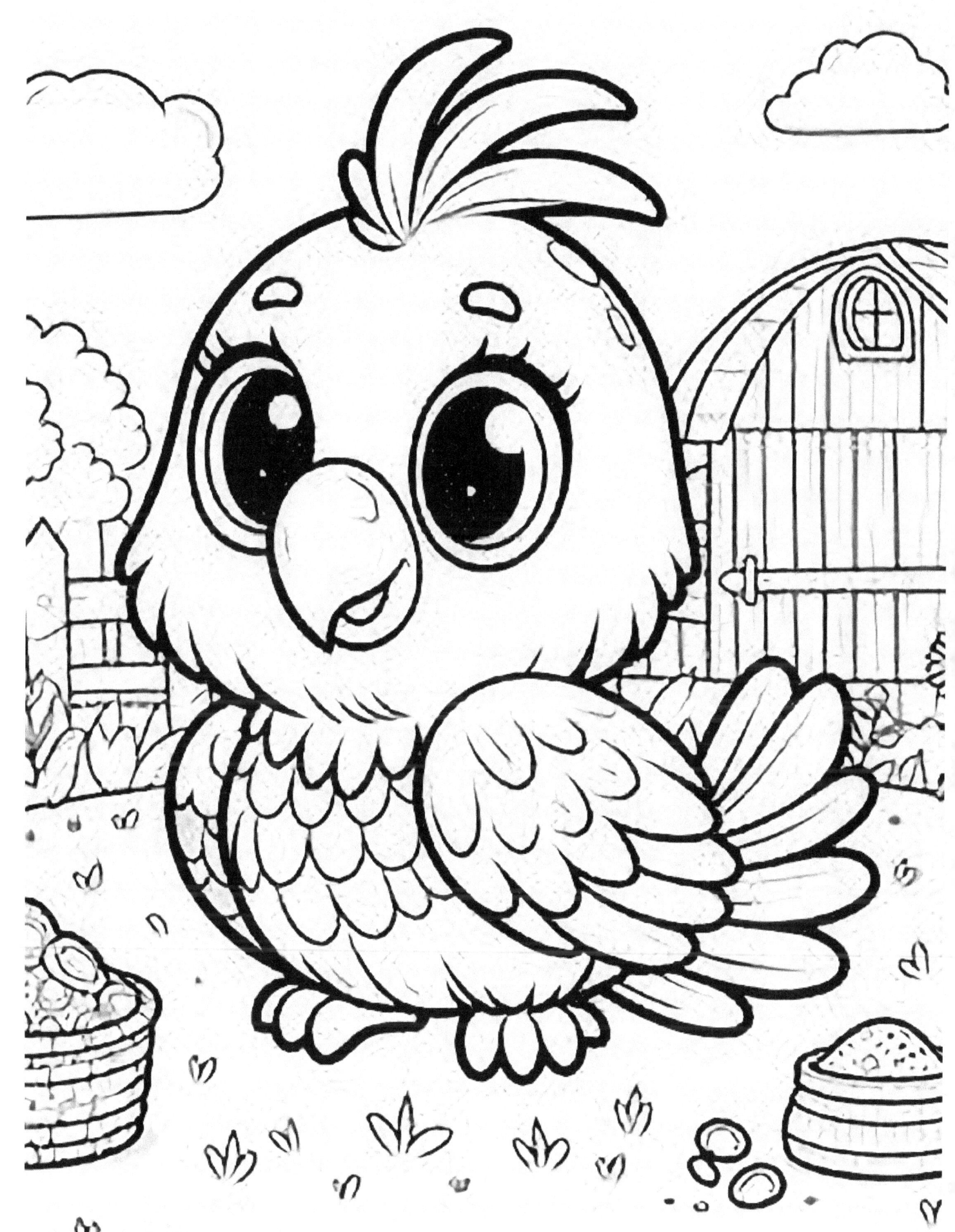

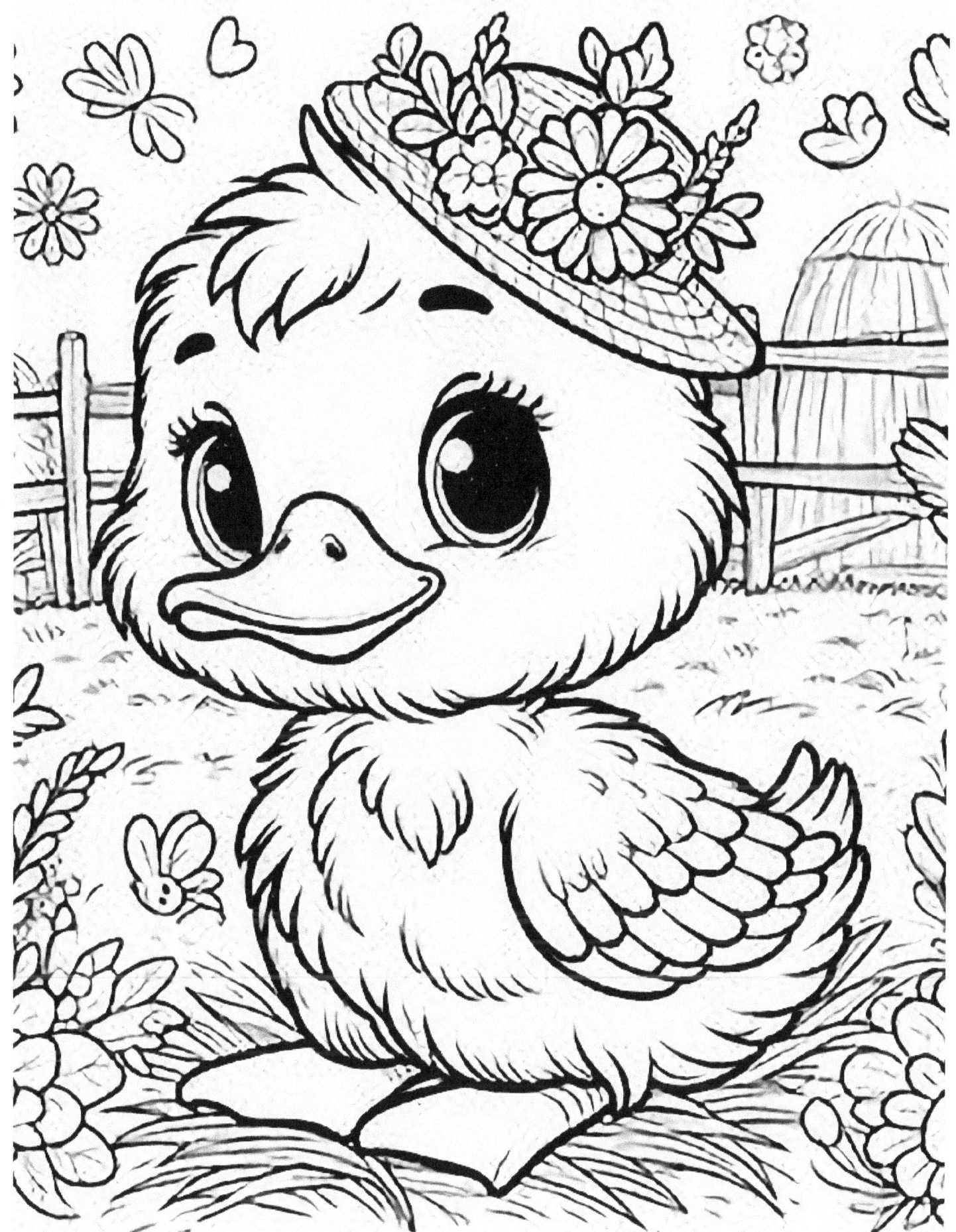

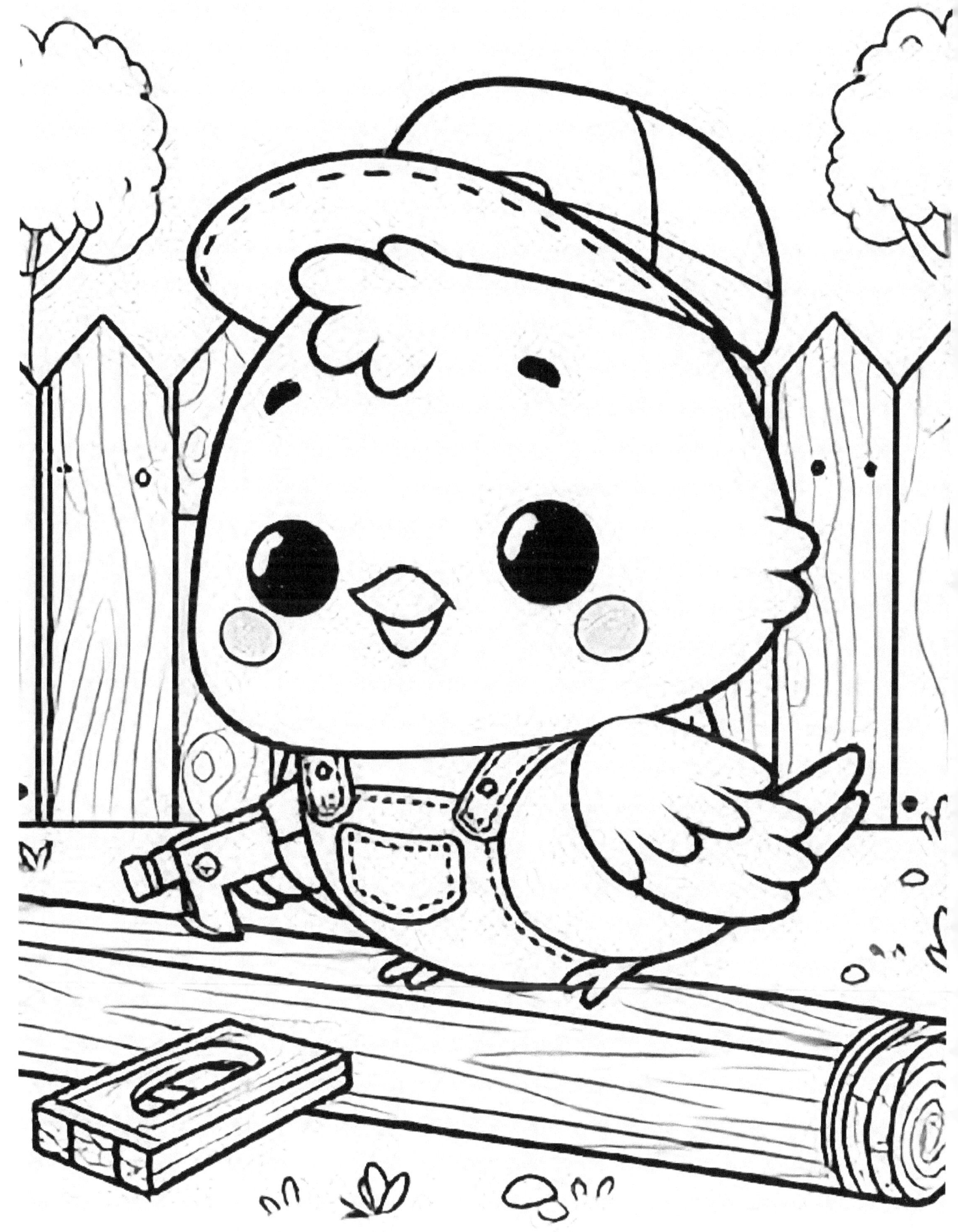

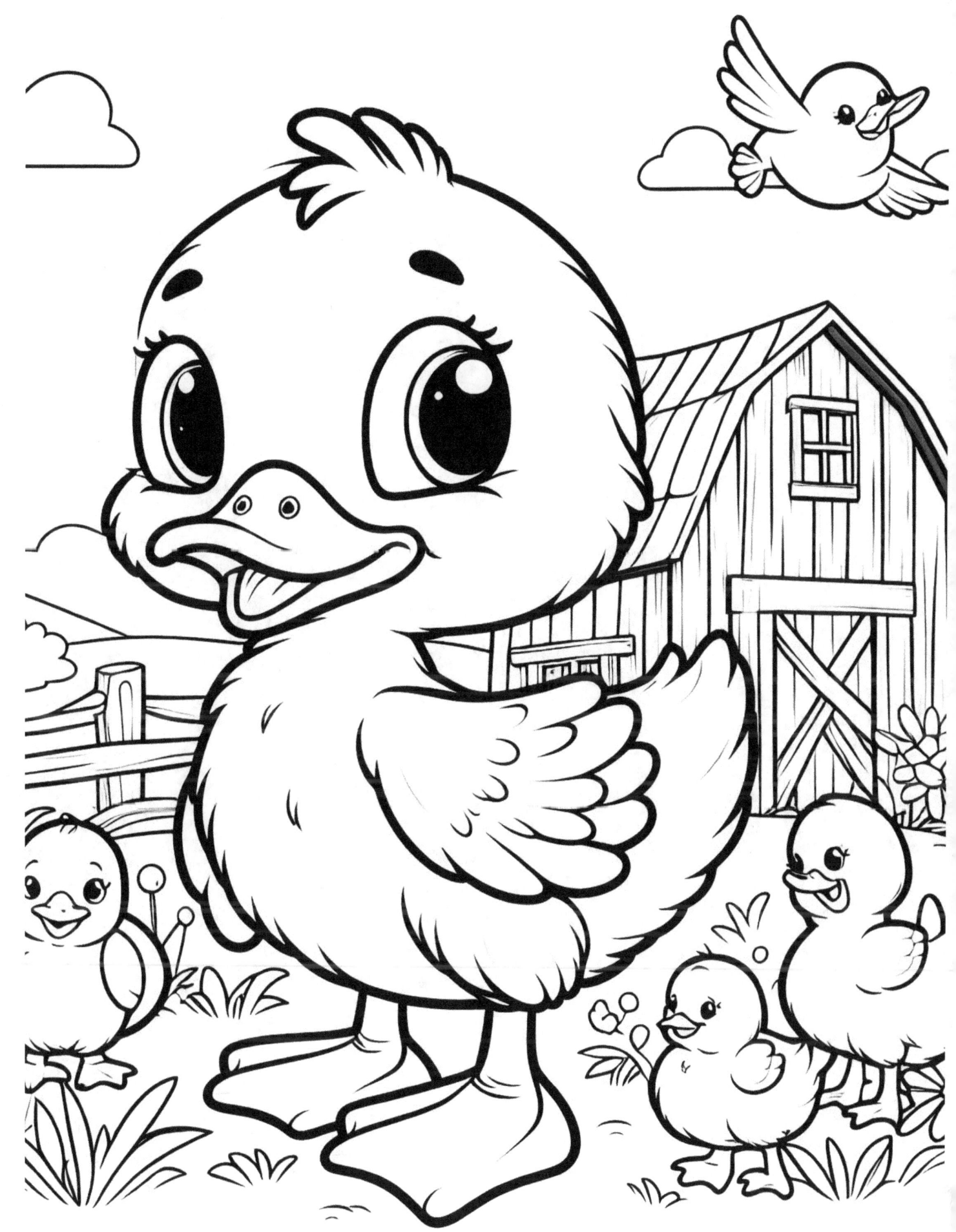

www.ingramcontent.com/pod-product-compliance
Lightning Source LLC
Chambersburg PA
CBHW080838310526
45796CB00015B/312